Pause to Think

PAUSE

TO THINK

USING MENTAL MODELS
to LEARN and DECIDE

JAIME LESTER

Columbia University Press
Publishers Since 1893
New York   Chichester, West Sussex

Library of Congress Cataloging-in-Publication Data
Names: Lester, Jaime (Investment consultant), author.
Title: Pause to think : using mental models to learn and decide / Jaime
Lester. Description: New York : Columbia University Press, 2024. |
Includes bibliographical references and index.
Identifiers: LCCN 2023053875 | ISBN 9780231212984 (hardback) |
ISBN 9780231559669 (ebook)
Subjects: LCSH: Decision making. | Cognitive maps (Psychology) |
Prejudices. | Perspective (Philosophy)
Classification: LCC BF448 .L478 2024 | DDC 153.8/3—dc23/eng/20240108
LC record available at https://lccn.loc.gov/2023053875

Cover design: Noah Arlow
Cover image: Shutterstock

For everyone who loves ideas, especially my wonderful family

Contents

Preface

've enjoyed reading books about mental models for decades, and my bookshelves are jammed full of them. Their pages are filled with psychological experiments that reveal the surprising outcomes that result from cognitive biases, which are both interesting and entertaining. There is also a small industry dedicated to providing mental model resources to aspiring learners: subscription websites, video courses, and of course, more books. Many of these promise to improve your intellect (and, by extension, your wealth and professional achievement) and offer either a bite of knowledge each day (via email) or an extensive survey that encompasses scores of models. I have sampled most of these offerings but remain unsatisfied.

This book introduces a different approach, a middle ground of sorts. I respect the scholarly study of mental models and the fascinating insights into human behavior that ensue from delving deeply into them. But I also understand that people's lives are busy, and something that will not be used is not useful. So, this book is structured to deliver a large amount of *usable* knowledge in as *short* and *memorable* a package as possible. As such, only thirty-two concepts are discussed—the ones that I believe are both the most important and broadly applicable. Exhaustive proof and documentary evidence are relegated to the footnotes and suggested readings—trust me but verify if you wish. And, most importantly, the concepts are rolled up into larger, actionable areas—decisions, learning, understanding, investing, and happiness. There is not an ounce of fat in this book—it is 100 percent lean muscle, designed to help you improve your intellectual and emotional lives. It is my sincere hope that the time you invest in reading this book and absorbing its contents will rank among the best-spent of your academic and professional careers.

That said, this book, like many aspects of life, can be seen both as an end and a beginning. For those readers seeking an efficient introduction to topics that will meaningfully impact their lives, this is the book for you.

For those readers seeking an introduction to the broad array of mental models as the launching point for a deeper and wider intellectual exploration, this book is also for you. For those readers who have no idea what mental models are or why they are important, hopefully this book will be for you as well!

If there is one overarching principle that you should take away from reading this book, it is that it is highly worthwhile to take the time to *pause to think*. *Pause* before making an important decision in order to implement a structured framework around it. *Pause* before learning something new to ascertain the most effective way of learning it. *Pause* before passing judgment until you understand all the cognitive biases at play. *Pause* when you are feeling unhappy to understand the roots of those feelings and how to actively counteract them. It doesn't have to be a long pause! But developing the habit of taking a small step back from the whirlwind of life will pay major dividends.

Let me start by defining these terms, as "mental model" is somewhat vague and can be used in different contexts. Any model is a simplification of reality that is employed to make a reasonable judgment, so it is helpful to further separate these ideas into concepts and frameworks. The term "important concepts" will be used for ideas that are significant enough to have broad application among various intellectual disciplines, and I will discuss thirty-two of these in the first part of the book. The term "important frameworks" will reflect the synthesis of these concepts with other ideas into actionable systems that will improve the efficiency and effectiveness of your thinking in different areas.

This book is organized in a fashion which hopefully you will find clear and concise. But just because it is short doesn't mean that the contents are simple—on the contrary. These are complicated and, at times, counterintuitive ideas, and you may need to think them through a few times to really grasp them. Hopefully, you will enjoy both the journey and the destination!

Part I. Important Concepts

Part II. Important Frameworks

Now, *pause*, take a breath, and let's get started!

Pause to Think

PART I

IMPORTANT CONCEPTS

1

Cognitive Biases

The human brain has evolved over many thousands of years to excel at certain tasks that improve its host's prospects for survival. As part of this process, our brains have developed mental shortcuts (also called heuristics) that increase decision-making speeds based on external stimuli. This was very helpful in Paleolithic times, when predators literally lurked around every corner, and can still be somewhat useful today. However, these same shortcuts can also lead to bad decisions and unintended outcomes in modern society. For instance, your hardwired instinct might be to treat anyone who looks different from you as a potential threat and react to them aggressively. Clearly, this approach is the wrong way to interact with strangers in most circumstances.

Moreover, evolution has given us brains that have developed in a haphazard manner. Let's use the model of a house that has been renovated on many separate occasions.[1] Central air conditioning was installed one year, while new pipes were installed another; a porch was added some years after that. Unfortunately, because of the way that the ducts were installed for the air conditioning, the pipes subsequently had to be installed on the outside of the house's walls. Now, if the weather gets cold enough, these pipes are at risk of freezing and bursting—a suboptimal design, to be sure! Similarly, each "renovation" of your brain helped your ancestors survive in some way: to more effectively avoid predators, find food, use tools, etc.

But the "renovations" were not purposefully designed (they happened by random mutation), and so while they usually function well together, sometimes these adaptations operate independently of each other, and occasionally they conflict massively. In other words, your brain is an incredibly powerful, highly complex, and randomly dysfunctional piece of equipment.

Another simplifying model is that the human brain has two separate systems for problem solving. The first is "fast" and developed earlier in our species' evolution—it rapidly arrives at decisions and is based mostly on instinct. The second system is "slow" and uses a more complex process to evaluate situations. It will usually reach a better answer to any given problem but will take a lot longer (and in a life-or-death situation, you may not have that time!). Additionally, the brain defaults to a "fast" thinking mode unless forced out of it, since it is still wired to use a survival mindset. Thus, if more time is available, it is frequently better to overrule this initial decision and apply the "slow" approach instead. Many of the recommendations in this book are based on replacing "fast" decisions with "slow" insights.

Most readers will remember an occasion where their immediate reaction to a situation was, with the benefit of hindsight, suboptimal. Perhaps it was a hastily composed email response, written while you were still angry, or an impulse purchase that you regretted soon after. Maybe it was the expression of a prejudice that didn't reflect your true feelings, or unnecessary verbal or physical aggression in a friendly basketball game. The brain's propensity to oversimplify and then act more quickly than necessary can be problematic.

This dynamic also applies over a longer time frame, as your brain reinterprets past events with its "oversimplification" filter. For example, many humans are overconfident—they believe that their ability to perform most activities is better than average, when in fact this is statistically impossible. Typically, people are average drivers, yet few of us think that we are.[2] This overconfidence stems from our brains' simplifications of past events, their causes, and their impacts on us—we ascribe good outcomes to skill and bad outcomes to luck. Tricking ourselves to increase our self-confidence may have improved chances of survival, but it still counts as self-delusion!

You may have watched online videos that show various riddles, optical illusions, and brain teasers that leave you quite confused.[3] The common thread that connects many of these is that the brain recognizes something that it has seen before (or so it thinks) and takes a shortcut to arrive at the answer. The problem is that these videos have introduced some nonobvious changes that significantly alter the outcome. The brain, in its race to get to the answer quickly, ignores these differences and then draws exactly the wrong conclusions! For example, if certn letrs r rmovd frm wrds, the brain will still "see" the whole word on a quick scan through the sentence and miss the spelling errors in the document.

Here are some examples of cognitive biases, but hundreds have been documented by thousands of scientific studies, demonstrating their existence and pervasiveness:

Overconfidence: People consistently believe that they are better than average at a wide range of activities, despite having no evidence to back this up.

Herd mentality/Social proof: People are most comfortable in the company of others. Even if someone knows that an answer is incorrect, they are still likely to choose that answer if surrounded by others who are also choosing it. This idea can also be applied to social norms—people will act in ways they know to be wrong if there are others around them acting the same way.

Loss aversion: People value losses and gains differently. As such, they are unlikely to undertake a profitable investment opportunity if it carries with it a high likelihood of loss. Similarly, people are unwilling to accept a sure loss and are willing to gamble at unfavorable odds to avoid this outcome.

Framing: People will interpret data based on how it is communicated (including verbal, visual, and contextual differences) instead of the information itself.

Anchoring: People use preexisting knowledge as a reference point. Any additional information is incorporated in relation to this point and can thus seem relatively good or bad depending on the anchor, even if the anchor itself is completely arbitrary.

Confirmation: People seek out that which confirms what they already believe and ignore or discount information that goes against their existing assumptions. This is done to reduce the stress of cognitive dissonance—the difficult act of holding contradictory ideas in one's mind at the same time.

Narrative fallacy: Humans prefer explanations that can be woven into coherent and compact stories to a messy and complicated reality. They will adhere to a story-based explanation, even when it is unlikely to be true.

Hindsight: People view outcomes in hindsight in ways that are most beneficial to them. This involves regretting decisions that led to poor outcomes, even if the decisions were optimal at the time they were made.

As previously mentioned, this also leads to the characterization of good outcomes as based on skill and therefore deserved, while bad outcomes are more frequently attributed to poor luck.

Availability and recency: People will give undue weight to recent and easily recalled data and experiences when making decisions, simply because they are freshest in their minds.

In each case, our brains misinterpret information and then act inappropriately as a result. Put differently, each of these biases is a description of how your mind will most likely act, unless you supervise it properly. Think of your brain as a child, who will make decisions without really thinking them through, unless you gently remind it to do otherwise. Just like children, sometimes brains need a time out (a *pause*, if you will)!

These concepts may sound somewhat abstract, but I would wager that you have experienced situations like the following, all of which can be traced back to one or more of these biases:

- A friend tells you about her excellent performance on a test, which she attributes to "how smart she is." She neglects to mention that the test was heavily focused on a chapter that she was fortunate to reread the night before class. (*Hindsight bias*)
- Your brother advises that you enroll your daughter in fencing classes, since his son just got into Dartmouth on a fencing scholarship. He doesn't mention that his son's friend, an equally accomplished fencer, did not get admitted. (*Confirmation bias*)
- You see a T-shirt in a store for $200 and think it is too costly. When you see the same shirt on sale for 75% off, you think it is reasonably priced, even though $50 for a T-shirt is . . . still quite expensive. (*Anchoring bias*)
- You are playing poker with your friends and lose $1,000. You are offered the following deal to help you "get out of the hole"—if the next card that is flipped over is a 10 or higher, you get your money back; otherwise, you owe another $1,000. You accept the poor odds, hoping to break even. (*Sure loss aversion*)
- Your daughter wants to go on a trip with her friends to Costa Rica. You refuse since half of the trip will be spent at a beach resort. However, she changes your mind, arguing that the other half will be spent building houses for low-income residents. (*Framing*)

– You ask a friend how much money is being raised for a business venture. She answers, "$1 billion." You ask about the worst possible outcome, such that if less than that is raised from investors, your friend would be obliged to chop off one of her own fingers. She replies that the lowest conceivable amount would be $500 million. On this basis, you join the company. The company ends up raising $25 million from investors. (*Overconfidence bias*)

As I previously mentioned, there have been thousands of psychological studies published that demonstrate these and hundreds of other mental biases. Reading long discussions of these studies, however, is not the best way to learn how to avoid them—it is simply too much information to remember! As you will learn in a later chapter, our brain functions best when it is able to organize large amounts of data into discrete categories, which is what I will do here. I submit that most cognitive biases can be traced back to one of three organizing principles:

– We like to feel good about ourselves.
– We interpret the world using stories instead of statistics.
– We make instinctive judgments and then stick to them.

Table 1.1 provides a list of many of the cognitive biases on Wikipedia, categorized into this simple framework.[4] If you visit the Wikipedia entry,

Table 1.1 Cognitive biases

Self-esteem	Stories (not statistics)	Snap judgments
Confirmation	Clustering	Anchoring
False consensus	Conjunction	Belief
Overconfidence	Base rate	Halo
Illusion of control	Probability neglect	Prospect
Dunning-Kruger	Hot hand	Attribution
Action	Framing	Availability
Hindsight	Berkson's paradox	Stereotyping
False uniqueness	Illusory correlation	Survivorship
Barnum	Duration neglect	Naïve realism
Disposition	Neglect of probability	Default
Endowment	Gambler's fallacy	Objectivity
Hard-easy	Effect	Outcome
Conformity	Subadditivity	Illusion of validity

you will see that there are more that I could have included here, but hopefully you get the point. There are also some biases that do not fit neatly into this framework, but not very many.

Remember the 3 S's:

Self-esteem
Stories (not statistics)
Snap judgments

If you can keep these categories in mind, while accepting that you are human and thus prone to each of these biases, then you will have taken a significant step toward eliminating these propensities.

It bears mentioning here that "you" and your brain are not the same. I will avoid engaging in a metaphysical discussion of what constitutes a "self," or whether the soul exists and/or resides within the human body. I am simply saying that within this framework of "fast" and "slow" mechanisms of thinking, you should consider your "slow" thoughts to be reflective of who you are as a person. It is natural to think of your brain and all the thoughts it produces as equivalent to your identity, ego, or other conception of personality. However, frequently your brain's "fast" mechanism produces thoughts that are judgmental, animalistic, or discriminatory. It is unpleasant to have these thoughts, and even though we usually reject them, their very presence can lead to negative feelings. We have all experienced this, and it is part of what makes us human. But the far greater indicator of our humanity is the fact that our "slow" brain kicks in to counteract these flawed mental processes.

Most of all, remember that your brain evolved in a way to benefit survival in a world that existed many millennia ago. This is not the same set of criteria that allows you to be happy, healthy, and successful in today's world. In fact, our brain's mechanisms specifically evolved to prevent us from getting too happy, since in prehistoric times this would have led to complacency and increased the odds of being eaten. Sunbathing cavemen probably didn't survive long enough to pass on their genetic material!

I'd like to make one final point here, addressed to the more skeptical readers. You may have noticed that I have made assertions without offering rigorous evidence. At least, I hoped you noticed this—being a critical thinker is a crucial skill! However, despite this dynamic, I am not asking you to simply take my word that these biases exist. While there are plenty of psychological studies that buttress these assertions, there is no need to prove or disprove anything at this juncture.[5] We simply need to acknowledge the following:

1. Many humans do have these biases (and many others), based on loads of experimental data and general experiences.
2. Since you are human, there is a decent chance that you, too, will make some of these same mistakes.
3. Being actively aware of these propensities may allow you to counteract them and avoid some unfortunate outcomes.
4. There is really no downside to keeping this in mind.

Now that we have finished our brief tour of cognitive biases, we can move on to other important concepts drawn from a variety of academic fields. As you will see, it was important to discuss these biases at the beginning of our journey, as they are interwoven into many aspects of our learning. It is even understandable that most books on mental models are devoted largely to this topic, given how interesting they are to consider and discuss. Still, they are just the start of our journey.

Remember to *pause to think* whether one of your biases is evidencing itself, or if you are using your "fast" thinking when you should use your "slow" approach. *Pause* after making a snap judgment to reconsider its logic. *Pause* before accepting a narrative at face value, and examine the data that corroborates it. And *pause* now to review the "3 S's" and implant them firmly in your brain!

2

The Humanities

Psychology, religion, and philosophy are three fields of study that share a common theme: they are each concerned with the ways in which we perceive ourselves, both individually and in relation to larger groups (our community or even all of humanity), and how we should behave as a result. These topics are clearly of great importance for our own emotional health, as well as that of society as a whole.

Religion and philosophy are fields that offer numerous recommendations that occasionally conflict with each other. For example, a branch of philosophy that focuses on individual rights will offer different advice than one that focuses on maximizing overall social benefit. A religion that preaches the importance of the universal acceptance of a single deity will lead its followers in a different direction than one that recommends broad tolerance of all beliefs. However, there are also many principles that are shared by most religions and philosophies, and we will focus on those.

Psychology can be both observational ("people seem to act in a certain way") and prescriptive ("this is how people *should* act or think"). It includes the study of the cognitive biases discussed in chapter 1 as well as much deeper and more complex patterns of thought and human behavior.

Logic is a field that has existed since ancient times and concerns itself with the study of correct reasoning. As such, it is no surprise that its ideas should have relevance to our discussion!

Finally, I draw upon the artistic world to provide us with the idea of perspective. Usually employed in realistic drawings, perspective connects the real world with our perception of it and shows how the two can frequently diverge. This distinction was hopefully illustrated in chapter 1 and will be a recurring theme in this book.

THE MIND-BODY CONNECTION

Discipline: Psychology

Summary: The mind and the body are fundamentally connected, and each influences the other's functioning.

Why it is important: Acknowledging that your physical health can be influenced by your mental health and that your mental functioning can be impaired by demands on your physical body is vital to living your best life.

Example in discipline: Research shows a strong connection between positive thinking and improved physical health.

Example outside discipline: Exercise encourages the production of growth factors, which can increase vasculature in the brain and the health of brain cells.

Discussion: It is tempting to regard one's mind and body as separate and distinct. Your mind "thinks" and tells your body what to do, and your body performs these actions and keeps your brain alive. They essentially operate in different spheres, overlapping only occasionally. However, the reality is much more complicated. Specifically:

1. *How you feel can change how you think.* Meditation can lead to enhanced cognitive performance and decision-making.[1]
2. *How you act can change how you feel.* The act of consciously smiling (even with no reason) will make you feel happier. Go ahead and smile, don't you feel better now?
3. *Your mind reacts to stress by releasing cortisol and other stress hormones.* These change how you feel, how you react to external stimuli, and may even shorten your life span.
4. *Sleep is more important than you might think.* Sleeping too little can both impair near-term cognitive function and reduce your expected life span (if it is a regular occurrence).
5. *The placebo effect can have as much or more impact on reducing pain than "real" medicine.* Take a moment to consider that—a fake ("sugar") pill can cure as much illness as a drug that takes billions of dollars and millions of hours to research and create. Our mind effectively just "heals" our body.[2]
6. *Mental feedback loops.* There are many feedback loops that include both psychological and physical processes—for example, getting nervous before public speaking causes one to sweat, and this sweat causes further nervousness.

7. *Pain is all in your mind.* The process of feeling "pain" is intermediated by the brain—sensory neurons fire, and this message is carried to the brain, which interprets it as "pain."
8. *You're only as old as you feel.* Seventy-five-year-old men who dressed and acted as though they were only fifty-five all showed improvement in measures of cognition, memory, and eyesight.[3] Think young!
9. *Get outside!* Your surroundings can also impact your stress levels and thought clarity. Walking in nature instead of an urban setting can reduce stress and negative thinking and improve overall mental health.

For these reasons, and many others, it is important to be aware of the interplay between physical and mental/emotional processes:

– It is likely that you have been, at one time or another, irritable due to hunger—"hangry," one might say.
– You may recently have been overly tired and thus unable to perform to your intellectual or physical potential.
– You may live or work in an environment that is causing you significant stress, which is having a serious physical and mental impact.

While we intuitively understand that sleep and hunger can affect us, we usually fail to appreciate the myriad of other ways in which our bodies and minds interact. To achieve peak achievement in either, we must pay attention to both.

Exercises:

1. Explain how being hungry, tired, or stressed can impact your physical performance or decision-making process.
2. There are people whose neurological systems function differently than most, such that they do not feel physical pain. Is this a benefit to them?
3. What is a "runner's high," and how does it help explain certain people's love of intense exercise?

UTILITARIANISM

Discipline: Philosophy

Summary: The morality of actions should be determined by that which provides the largest overall benefit to the most people.

Why it is important: In most cases, a morally reasonable approach will maximize the overall benefit to society. There are important exceptions to this rule, but it has broad applicability to both small and large groups, including a firm's customers and employees.

Example in discipline: Standing next to a track switch, you see that a trolley is heading toward a group of children, who are tied to the tracks ahead of it (figure 2.1). You could switch the trolley to another set of tracks, saving the lives of the children, but killing an innocent man. Utilitarianism

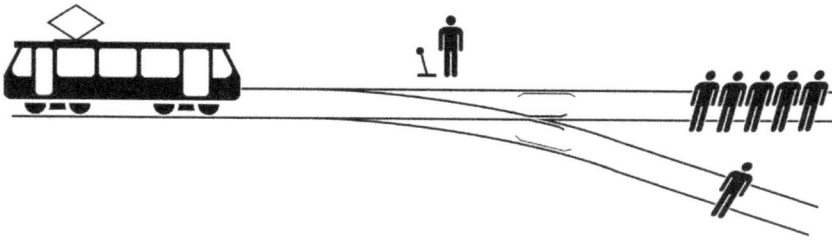

FIGURE 2.1 The trolley problem. Courtesy of McGeddon via Wikimedia Commons, CC BY-SA 4.0. https://commons.wikimedia.org/wiki/File:Trolley_problem.png.

states that you should take this action, as it would lead to a greater number of lives being saved.

Example outside discipline: You have an umbrella that can shelter three people. You are walking in one direction, being kept dry by the umbrella. You see three people walking in the opposite direction, getting wet. You should offer them your umbrella (and hope that they will return it after the rainstorm), since keeping three people dry is better than one.

Discussion: Most famously discussed by Jeremy Bentham in the late 1700s, utilitarianism posits that acting to maximize benefits to the largest number of people is the fairest way to make decisions. If twenty people want to go to the movies and only five want to go to the park, it is probably reasonable for the group to go to the movies. However, this approach must also be tempered with respect for individual members of the group and the benefit or harm they will feel in each of the outcomes. For instance, if the movie is extremely scary and one member of the group will have nightmares for a month, it is not fair to make that person watch the movie. There is not one simple answer— each situation is complex, since people's needs and emotions are complicated.

From a purely rational basis, utilitarianism seems like an attractive moral philosophy. Unfortunately, it makes no allowances for basic human rights or justice. Taken to its logical extreme, relying on utilitarianism can lead to some highly immoral (or amoral[4]) outcomes. It is for this reason that modern philosophers have blended utilitarianism principles with a fundamental presumption of the importance of human rights. For example, John

Rawls proposed a version of utilitarianism where an action is moral if it both maximizes happiness AND every individual is better off than before the action.

In business, utilitarianism is an unwritten rule that guides many decisions. Resources are targeted toward markets based on their size and potential. Profit maximization demands that investment capital is directed toward its most productive uses. Human resources decisions are generally made based on what benefits the greatest number of employees. However, successful businesses must also respond to the individual needs of their customers or employees, understanding that the inefficiency that results is more than offset by the benefit to the firm's culture and reputation.

Exercises:

1. Here are ranked preferences for what your friends want to do this evening. Which do you think provides the best utilitarian outcome, and why?

	Bowling	Ping pong	Movie
Judy	1	2	3
Pat	1	3	2
Dan	3	2	1
Bill	3	2	1

2. In which of these situations would utilitarianism probably be the wrong system for deciding on the best outcome?

   a. Sacrificing a human each year to a god so that she brings good weather for your crops.
   b. Knocking down a small apartment building in order to build a state-of-the-art hospital.
   c. Taking half of people's savings to redistribute them to poorer citizens.
   d. Rationing end-of-life medical care to pay for vaccinations.

3. Utilitarianism is applicable not just to decisions made for large groups of people or whole societies, but whenever there are scarce resources. How might you apply utilitarianism to putting together a grocery list if you only have $50 to spend for a week of food?

HIERARCHY OF NEEDS

Discipline: Psychology/Religion

Summary: Human happiness is dependent on many factors. Some of these are basic, like food and water. But other needs are also important, such as being in loving relationships and deriving satisfaction from professional and personal achievements.

Why it is important: Humans have basic needs that are required to prevent suffering—food, air, water, and shelter. However, emotional needs must also be satisfied if we are to have a chance of experiencing happiness, and this concept explores some of those needs.

Example in discipline: Psychology as an academic discipline concerns itself with the workings of the human mind and behavior. This is one model for understanding human happiness and motivation.

Example outside discipline: People can be satisfied easily at first (think of a child and a new toy), but it takes more and more to do so as time goes on. Part of this is habituation—the human mind "resets" the levels of accomplishment that must be reached to effect a chemical stimulus—and part of it is a biological drive to achieve and accomplish. Higher-level needs are usually more difficult to achieve. Most (but not all) people in the United States are well-fed and have shelter, but far fewer have high self-esteem and a real sense of self-actualization (the fulfillment of one's potential).

Discussion: Abraham Maslow proposed this theory of human motivation in 1943. He thought that each of the levels of a pyramid had to be satisfied before the next could be addressed, which seems not to be strictly true. This "hierarchy of needs" parallels human development (i.e., children's brains as they mature) and has found application in various business and civic areas (figure 2.2). For example, consider the question of employee motivation structures: Is money enough, or are other aspects such as responsibility and respect just as important? Research indicates the latter. The framework is also similar to that described by Hinduism, which teaches that while humans are satisfied with food or physical objects at first, they ultimately require intellectual and spiritual motivation to be fulfilled.

This concept dovetails nicely with the logical construct of "necessary versus sufficient." For example, oxygen is necessary for a fire to burn, but it is not sufficient—fuel and a spark are also needed. Food is necessary for human happiness, but it also is not sufficient—love, safety, and a sense of achievement are also required. It is important to focus on the necessary,

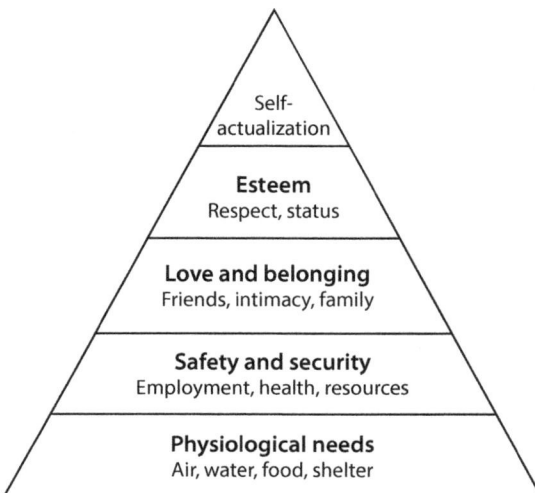

Self-actualization

Esteem
Respect, status

Love and belonging
Friends, intimacy, family

Safety and security
Employment, health, resources

Physiological needs
Air, water, food, shelter

FIGURE 2.2 Hierarchy of needs.

such as earning enough money to pay bills, but also to remember that this is not sufficient—it is instead just part of a larger picture.

Exercises:

1. Aside from food, water, sleep, and shelter, name three things without which you could not live.
2. Many religious followers intentionally ignore their physical needs or cravings to focus on their spiritual development. How does this fit in with Maslow's framework?
3. Many careers also have a hierarchy of learning—for example, doctors must go through college, medical school, general medical training, and specialized medical training. Do you think that career satisfaction necessarily increases as your training and capability do?

THE GOLDEN RULE

Discipline: Ethics/religion

Summary: The Golden Rule states that one should treat others as one would like to be treated.

Why it is important: This near-universal maxim of human behavior is a powerful precept to consult when determining the morality of one's actions.

Example in discipline: In 400 BC, the Greek orator Isocrates wrote, "Do not do to others that which angers you when they do it to you." Every major religion has since incorporated this teaching in some capacity.

Example outside discipline: Tim used to leave dishes in the employee break room for others to load into the dishwasher. Then Tim realized that he wouldn't like cleaning up after his coworkers and decided that he should change his behavior.

Discussion: The study of moral reasoning involves the creation of fundamental rules that guide our understanding of how to live a virtuous life (such as "Do not kill"). However, these rules can vary significantly among branches of philosophy. For instance, many believe that it is fine to kill animals if it aids human survival (for example, in pharmaceutical trials), while others disagree. Some might think it is preferable for one person to die instead of one hundred (utilitarianism), while others would argue that no life should be knowingly sacrificed. The Golden Rule seems to be largely accepted by most religions and philosophies and is largely uncontroversial.

The Golden Rule is based on a highly intuitive and simple premise: "I should not do anything to someone else that harms that person. A reasonable way to decide if the action is harmful is whether I would want it done to me." While this rule may lack nuance, in general it is a good starting point for considering moral and philosophical questions.

Hopefully, you are not in the habit of mistreating others and this rule is second nature. However, I suspect that you have frequently been highly critical of yourself after experiencing some failure, small or large. To a certain extent, this is human nature. If you invert[5] the precept, though, you will see that it is in fact moral to:

"Treat yourself the way that you treat others."

In other words, don't be harder on yourself than you would be on a friend or coworker. If someone you know made a mistake, you would likely demonstrate empathy and forgiveness, and perhaps try to help them not to repeat that mistake. You probably wouldn't write them off and judge them to be a terrible person. In a work environment, if a colleague made an isolated honest error, you might be disappointed but would likely move past it quickly. Remember to be similarly lenient with yourself when you make comparable mistakes!

Exercises:

1. How might you reword the Golden Rule if you are trying to communicate it to a kindergartner?
2. Does following the Golden Rule make sense in real life if other people are not following it?
3. How do cultural differences figure into the conception of the Golden Rule? Do most societies have a similar enough system of values that the rule can be applied across cultures?

RECIPROCITY

Discipline: Psychology

Summary: Reciprocity is the human inclination to return good behavior and punish bad behavior.

Why it is important: As one of the most strongly followed social norms, reciprocity comes into play in a variety of circumstances. Recognizing when it is being employed and when to employ it yourself can be a powerful tool.

Example in discipline: In an early experiment, a researcher sent holiday cards to hundreds of random strangers. Most of these people sent holiday cards back, many with handwritten notes.

Example outside discipline: Charities will frequently send free gifts to prospective donors—mailing labels, tote bags, holiday cards, or pens. Once these gifts are received and accepted, people feel guilty if they don't donate.

Discussion: The human brain developed in ways that rewarded positive group behavior. Helping another member of your group survive— by hunting together, defending against attacks, or sharing shelter— would be repaid later. As a result, there was an evolutionary benefit to those with a genetic disposition to perform and return favors, as their groups would cooperate effectively to improve prospects of survival. For our current species, this tendency is now hardwired—most people feel guilty if they don't reciprocate another's generosity.

Much like the Golden Rule, reciprocity appeals to one's sense of fairness, a powerful force that develops when we are young children. Taking something and then not repaying the act seems unfair, which feels wrong to us. While we intuitively know (and are reminded by our parents) that life isn't fair, nonetheless we still believe that it *should* be.[6]

Of course, this tendency can be preyed upon. An unscrupulous person can trick others into acting against their best interests by creating a sense of reciprocity. Family members, coworkers, or other professional contacts may perform an unsolicited "favor" and then expect special treatment in return. Even the aforementioned charities are wasting significant resources (pens, bags, labels, and postage) to guilt people into donating money. Understanding this and absolving yourself of any responsibility to reciprocate can let you make decisions that are in your best interest, without an artificial sense of obligation.

Exercises:

1. A man on the street hands you a small trinket, then refuses to take it back, asking for a donation instead. He seems very nice. What do you do?
2. A friend lends you money so that you don't get evicted from your apartment. You pay her back. Later, she asks you to store a large bag of what appear to be illegal drugs, since "you owe her." What do you do?
3. Why do (typically) men buy women drinks at a bar? Is there an inherent expectation or social contract associated with that behavior?

OCCAM'S RAZOR

Discipline: Logic

Summary: The simpler the explanation, the more likely it is to be correct.

Why it is important: Frequently, the best answers are the ones that are the most obvious. It is best to simplify where possible instead of unnecessarily complicating one's analysis.

Example in discipline: Albert Einstein's theory of special relativity, Charles Darwin's theory of evolution, and Max Planck's quantum theory all relied on some simplification of assumptions, or "parsimony" as it is called in the scientific literature.

Example outside discipline: A hairy animal that leaves large tracks in the mud is much more likely to be a bear than a yeti.[7]

Discussion: In the history of ideas, there are many famous examples where complex explanations lost out to simpler ones. The geocentric model of the universe (Ptolemy) was replaced with a heliocentric model (Copernicus) because the calculations became much simpler—and they were simpler because they were correct! However, this is not to say that simple ideas are always correct—Newtonian physics lost out to Einstein's theory of relativity, for example.

Perhaps a better formulation of Occam's razor would be that you should simplify wherever possible, but not just for the sake of simplifying. As Einstein is said to have put it: "Everything should be kept as simple as possible, but not simpler." You can extend this approach from the theoretical to the practical—finishing tasks (at home and at work), creating art and literature, and even making decisions are all activities that suffer from the introduction of the unnecessary and the superfluous. Instead, adopt the U.S. Navy's design principle of "Keep It Simple, Stupid"!

This concept has strong ties to probability—simple explanations are statistically more likely. Adding multiple conditions to an explanation (to make it better fit the evidence) also introduces additional probabilities that these conditions are false, thus making it less likely that the overarching explanation is correct (this is just a mathematical truism—we will discuss probability a bit later in the book). For example, a plane that crashes due to a simultaneous failure of two parts at the same time as gale-force winds is the coincidence of three unlikely events. The chances of this happening are minuscule (say, $1/1,000 \times 1/1,000 \times 1/1,000$, which is one in a billion), while pilot error is a simpler and therefore much higher-probability explanation.

Corollary: Hanlon's Razor

This maxim states that one should never attribute to malice that which can be attributed to stupidity. In other words, if someone does something that you find distasteful or inappropriate, you should give them the benefit of the doubt at first. Maybe they just made a dumb mistake. Maybe they have a reasonable explanation for acting in that manner (for example, driving recklessly because they need to get to the hospital). While they could also just be a terrible person, it is generally best to resort to this explanation only after all others have been exhausted.

Exercises:

1. You have been running every day for the last week. You develop a pain in your leg, which could potentially be the manifestation of a bone tumor. Should you have an X-ray taken to make sure?
2. "Elegant" mathematical proofs or computer code are those that solve a problem parsimoniously or with a minimum amount of effort. Why is this especially important in those fields?
3. What is the highest-probability explanation for a late homework assignment—the dog ate it, it was damaged due to a water leak in one's house, or the student forgot to do it?

INVERSION

Discipline: Logic

Summary: Problems are sometimes more easily solved by working backward or "inverting" them.

Why it is important: Frequently, the path to success lies in avoiding that which causes failure and not overcomplicating the process.

Example in discipline: If the statement "All mirrors are shiny" is true, then the inverse statement, "If it is not shiny, then it is not a mirror," is also true.

Example outside discipline: A company that is trying to increase the job satisfaction of its workers will consider all the factors that contribute to dissatisfaction (low pay, lack of purpose, lack of responsibility, absence of growth opportunities, etc.) and then try to minimize those factors.

Discussion: It seems natural to start at the cause and end at the effect, but problem-solving isn't always linear. Frequently, we can more easily discern the cause by examining the effect and then interpolating between the two.

An alternate way to understand inversion is that we are considering the counterfactual, or "What if?" On a personal note, I'm a mediocre basketball player and have a lot of room for improvement. What sort of characteristics do bad basketball players have? They dribble with their head down, play lazy defense, and don't have a consistent shooting form, among others. Am I guilty of any of these? Why yes, all of them in fact, and I am working to minimize each of them.[8]

For many pursuits, consistency is a key contributor to success, and inversion helps us improve this trait. The absence of errors almost always triumphs over the presence of brilliance in fields as diverse as athletics, business, academia, and investing. Inversion allows us to see what bad habits must be purged to achieve this desired consistency.

Inversion also alerts you to risks that you might not consider. The concept of the "premortem" encourages you to anticipate various ways that you might fail, as well as the reasons for the failure. Then, you can strive to avoid those pitfalls! Charlie Munger, Warren Buffet's long-time business partner and one of the most famous proponents of inversion, is quoted as saying, "All I want to know is where I'm going to die, so I'll never go there." Charlie almost made it to one hundred, so the approach worked, but not perfectly!

While this concept may not resonate, or it may seem to be less useful than others, we will return to this approach regularly in the frameworks section (Part II) of this book. As I have found, once you start considering that avoiding a negative is better than chasing a positive, you can't get the idea out of your head!

Exercises:

1. What are some ways a company's marketing department could use inversion to improve their advertising campaign?
2. How will researching the most common causes of relationship failures enable you to strengthen your marriage?
3. How can inversion improve your financial health?

PERSPECTIVE

Discipline: Art

Summary: Interpretation of a situation can vary dramatically depending on one's physical or intellectual vantage point.

Why it is important: All external information is processed through the human brain, and the way in which this occurs can be somewhat arbitrary. There are few absolute truths in our world but rather multitudes of different perspectives on the same set of facts. Remember to consider how your circumstances shape your viewpoints and appreciate others' varying experiences as well.

Example in discipline: A small object viewed from up close appears large, while a large object seems tiny when seen from far away.

Example outside discipline: Disappointment from failure will usually fade as you realize that it is not all that bad or meaningful; as you "keep things in perspective," so to speak.

Discussion: A famous *New Yorker* cover once portrayed New York City as the center of the world, with other states and countries vanishing into nothingness in relation.[9] This illustration captured not only the physical reality of perspective—that objects in the distance appear smaller—but also the emotional reality that humans are inexorably shaped by their development and upbringing. The same set of facts can be interpreted in diametrically opposed manners, as individuals view them through the lenses of their own opinions, norms, biases, and belief systems. For example, a rambunctious child could either be a symbol of parental failure, a celebration of the freedom of youth, or both!

This is both problematic and wonderful. Problematic since human conflict is frequently exacerbated by these disparate viewpoints, but wonderful since it brings a richness of experience and the ability to walk in someone else's shoes. There is an old story about five blind men encountering an elephant for the first time, and each touching a different part. As a result, one feels its sharp tusk and believes that it is dangerous, another grasps its small tail and considers it puny, a third holds the trunk and believes that an elephant is a type of snake, and so on. The parable is meant to illustrate the diversity of opinion and respect for perspective, as each man had reason to believe what he did. But each man was ultimately wrong in his assessment, as he could not appreciate the whole. In other words, while it is important to understand and appreciate the perspectives of others, it is also vital to zoom out far enough from a situation that its true nature can be revealed.

As when viewing art, when you are too close to something you may not be able to properly judge its importance. Taking a step back, literally and figuratively, will help give context and allow for mitigating understanding.

Being passed over for a promotion may hurt badly at the time but is unlikely to meaningfully impact your career trajectory over the span of several decades. The experience may also spur you to upgrade your skill set and allow for greater success in the future. Framing the situation as a positive learning experience instead of an example of failure (i.e., the satisfaction of overcoming an obstacle instead of bemoaning its existence) can also have a beneficial impact on your mental health (thinking back to the *mind-body connection*).[10]

While the word "perspective" originated in the 1300s and was related to the science of optics, the roots of the word literally mean "to look through." As such, you should not be surprised to hear that synonyms include attitude, context, mindset, viewpoint, and frame of reference, all words that convey a mind's interpretation of external events. And of course, a trite but important example of perspective change is viewing a glass as half-full instead of half-empty.

The concept of perspective can be applied in a few different ways. An "inside" view takes a situation and tries to understand it in isolation based on its idiosyncratic fact pattern. An "outside" view tries to find similar situations or data, and predict outcomes based on this larger class of examples—effectively, a statistical analysis. Both can be helpful, as all situations have both similarities and differences with their predecessors. Research (and common sense) indicate that if skill plays a large role in determining an activity's outcome, then the "inside" view should be given a larger weight, and vice versa if luck does.[11]

The term "historiography" refers to the study of history and the differences among different historical writings about the same event. Despite what we were taught as children, history is not simply an impartial summary of facts and events. Instead, it is shaped by its writers—those who won the wars, civilizations that triumphed over others, and governments' officially sanctioned accounts. One must keep in mind when reading history that there are always other perspectives that are not being represented.

Other idioms spring to mind as well. Taking a "ten-thousand-foot view" can be appropriate for absorbing the complete picture, but it can deny a detailed understanding of the situation. On the other hand, "getting lost in the weeds" indicates that you are "missing the forest for the trees" and losing sight of a larger perspective by getting bogged down by the details. "Thinking big" is great, unless you are thinking too big! It kind of makes you wonder, "Why are there so many cliches about perspective?"

Exercises:

1. Self-help gurus suggest replacing the phrase "I have to" with "I get to," as in, "I get to drive my child to soccer practice." Why might this be a useful exercise?
2. How is your perspective related to your expectations about your career, family, or physical health?
3. The TV show *Undercover Boss* featured CEOs working incognito at their companies. Why might this be a valuable exercise for CEOs in general?

3

Investing and Science

Many of the cognitive biases discussed earlier in this book have their roots in investment research, specifically the field of "behavioral finance" that developed in the 1970s. Before then, economics and financial market researchers had assumed that market participants were rational, mathematically literate, and solely focused on optimizing their investment returns. As experiments showed that human beings were in fact frequently irrational, poor at math, and incapable of predicting which outcomes would be best for them, the profession had to reluctantly acknowledge that their neat mathematical models did not capture reality well after all.

While much of finance is, in fact, grounded in basic mathematics (the price of a bond, for instance, is usually precisely and accurately calculated by a single formula), there are also massive price fluctuations that are determined by human psychology and emotion. Some of these factors cause investors to make consistently poor investment decisions—and currently allow quantitative or computer-driven models to profit from taking the other side of these poor choices.

The fact is that even with billions of dollars on the line, most people cannot change basic inclinations that they know, rationally, to be flawed.[1] This indicates how powerful these biases are, which you should keep in mind as you undertake your journey to rid yourself of these same biases— the journey will not be without its challenges!

Aside from finance, the concepts in this chapter come from science—biology, chemistry, physics, medicine, and engineering. The scientific method may be the single best tool for seeking out truth in our world, and it should not be surprising that applying scientific concepts can play a large role in thinking more effectively.

EXPECTATIONS

Discipline: Investing

Summary: Success or failure is not determined by an absolute result, but by the result relative to expectations around it.

Why it is important: Most facets of human life have expectations incorporated into them. Success, happiness, satisfaction, and even stock prices all reflect this dynamic, and as such it is vital to explicitly understand.

Example in discipline: Meta reported quarterly revenues of $6 billion, which reflected growth of 25 percent versus the year-earlier period. While this was healthy, investors expected 30 percent growth, and as a result Meta stock declined significantly after the report.

Example outside discipline: You are excited to see a new movie, which has opened to rave reviews. Many of your friends have told you that it is one of the best movies they have ever seen. You watch it and, while you find it enjoyable, you don't think it lived up to the hype. As a result, you watched an excellent movie, yet you were disappointed by the experience, as your expectations were set too high ahead of time.

Discussion: It is natural to think in absolute terms, but most of the world operates on a relative basis. Your wealth, grades, and height don't convey satisfaction on their own, but are instead compared to friends' and colleagues' to determine your relative standing within your peer group.[2] As we will see in our discussion of happiness in chapter 10, this lens of relativity is frequently a source of dissatisfaction, as we constantly judge ourselves against our closest peers (and find ourselves lacking in some areas), instead of appreciating our absolute positions.

In investing, expectations play a significant role in price fluctuations, so much so that fund managers, policy makers, and corporate management teams all actively manage investors' expectations as part of their jobs. In real life, expectations might be even more important. This is true across the board, and applies to:

- Expectations that you have for others.
- Expectations that others have for you.
- Expectations that you have for yourself.

It is vital to recognize that performance relative to expectations usually matters much more than the absolute result. A heavily favored Olympic athlete will be devastated if she "only" wins the silver medal, despite being the second-best athlete in the world at that sport.[3] A successful career as a teacher will be highly satisfying, unless you had always expected that, one day, you would be president of the United States. And you might be very happy with meatloaf for dinner, unless you had anticipated Taco Tuesday.

It is also important to recognize that in most circumstances you have formed expectations, whether they are explicitly acknowledged or not. Since these expectations are likely in place, and your satisfaction will be determined relative to them, it is crucial that you make these *implicit* expectations into *explicit* ones. If you do not undertake this process, then it will be very difficult to understand the root cause of your feelings of joy or disappointment. Let me expand on this point, as it is so important.

In most facets of your life, you will have expectations around your level of achievement. This encompasses everything from grades and academic success to athletic ability and social status, and further extends to personal and professional accomplishments. Whether you are forming these expectations yourself, your parents or bosses are forming them for you, or society has imposed them on you without your explicit approval, they exist. If you fall short of those expectations, you will feel unhappy (or worse), and if you were not previously honest with yourself about holding these expectations, you may not even understand why. It will just be an unpleasant feeling in the pit of your stomach, which may eventually be unearthed by a talented psychotherapist.

The best way to avoid this situation is to move these expectations from an unexamined state to one of conscious appraisal. That way, if you do fall short, you will understand your disappointment and be able to deal with it head-on. And, even more importantly, you will be able to question these expectations ahead of time and decide whether they are reasonable, reflect your current priorities, and allow you to live your best life. If they do not, you can and should adjust them accordingly!

Similarly, it is important to have clear expectations of all aspects of your work and the work of those you manage. Are the criteria for bonuses and promotions clearly laid out, and does everyone involved understand them? As someone who has been on both ends of bonus discussions that involved unmet expectations, I can strongly attest to the importance of this process. Note that I am not opining on the process of setting goals or targets, and how ambitious to make them—every firm has its own strategy around this and other incentive structures. I am just pointing out that implicit expectations run the risk of harming working relationships when they are unmet, especially when a financial penalty can result.

Exercises:

1. Tesla reported its quarterly results, and the press release seemed negative, as earnings dropped 50 percent. However, the stock price increased 20 percent that day. Why might that be?

2. You study hard for a test and believe you know the material very well. You got 90 percent and were disappointed. You barely study for your next test and expect to do badly. You get 90 percent and are elated. What explains this?

3. A friend is cooking dinner for you. You have heard that he is an excellent cook and are excited to see for yourself. However, he warns you ahead of time that he is missing some ingredients and the dish will suffer as a result. However, when you taste it, you think it is wonderful. Additionally, you suspect that he was not, in fact, missing any ingredients. What was your friend likely doing?

RISK VERSUS REWARD

Discipline: Investing

Summary: Risk is usually understood as losses that result when a negative outcome occurs, though it can be defined in many ways. Reward, in contrast, is the benefit that one expects to receive with a good outcome. It is the relative *magnitudes* and *likelihoods* of these good and bad outcomes that determine the attractiveness of an investment.

Why it is important: Focusing only on risk makes you afraid to ever act; focusing only on reward reveals you as naïve. The reality is that almost all decisions should consider both, and it is the relative amount of each that allows you to determine whether to move ahead.

Example in discipline: You can invest in a project where you make a 15 percent return if it goes well (reward) and lose 50 percent of your money if it goes badly (risk). As you view these outcomes as equally likely, you do not make the investment, judging that the risk/reward is not favorable.

Example outside discipline: You are considering leaving your stable job for a founding role at a startup. The risk of the move would be a significant pay cut, while the reward would be equity ownership in a potentially valuable firm. You deem the improved work environment as roughly offset by the higher stress that the new job brings with it. Since the likelihood of success of the startup is low, and hence the expected value of your equity is also low, you decide to stay at your current job.

Discussion: There are many ways to define risk, but here it is meant as the potential downside of a decision. In financial terms, it is how much you can lose if an investment performs badly. In real terms, it is the potential negative consequences—financial, reputational, professional, emotional, or physical—of a choice that knowingly involves the chance of harm or loss. Reward is joined to risk's proverbial hip: What is the benefit or upside if a situation turns out well? Is it high enough to compensate for the downside risk, or is it too low, in which case you should not move forward?

It is the intersection of risk and reward that determines whether an investment is attractive. Many great investors will happily make an investment that has only a very small potential upside if they also believe it has virtually no downside (like cash in a savings account). Similarly, there are wonderful investments that have tremendous upside but potentially risk the loss of the entire investment amount.[4] The investments to avoid, of course, are those that entail both high risk and low reward—stay away!

This holds for life as well (shocking, I know—are you sensing a pattern?). It is always beneficial to seek out situations that have great upside (reward) and low downside (risk). One example might be taking a job at a startup when you are fresh out of business school, so the worst-case scenario is that you learn a new skill and work in an exciting environment, while the best case (even if it is unlikely) is that you are an early employee at a highly valued and successful enterprise. A situation to avoid, conversely, is lending your car to an untrustworthy friend—the best-case scenario is that you get your car back in one piece, while there are many potential downside outcomes to be considered.

Of course, you won't know the exact probabilities of each outcome when you make the decision, so you need to form your best estimates using the information you have at the time. Also, a caveat—it is usually easier to quantify risk than reward, so you should not be scared away from a decision simply because the risks are initially more obvious. Take the time to think through the rewards, and then make the best decision you can.

Exercises:

1. Which is a better investment—investing $100 with a 50 percent chance of doubling your money and a 50 percent chance of losing 25 percent, or investing $100 with a 10 percent chance of making ten times your money and a 90 percent chance of losing it all?
2. How would you think about the "risk" of going to law school?
3. You look at an investment and decide that the reward is not worth the risk. Your friend looks at the same situation and comes to the opposite conclusion. What might explain this?

COMPOUND INTEREST

Discipline: Investing

Summary: Compound interest refers to interest that is paid not only on the original amount of the investment (principal), but also on the interest that has accrued from previous periods.

Why it is important: Albert Einstein once called compound interest "the eighth wonder of the world" so that's got to count for something! Interest that gets paid over long periods of time accumulates at a geometric rate, and geometric growth accelerates over time. One dollar that compounds at 20 percent per year would turn into over $9,000 (you

Table 3.1 Value of retirement savings over time

Age when savings begins	Value of $1,000 at retirement
20	$90,017
30	$33,115
40	$12,182
50	$4,482

read that correctly) after 50 years, the average length of a career. Finding an investment that returns 20 percent (after tax) for half a century is, of course, the tricky part.

Example in discipline: Bob knows that saving for retirement is more effective the earlier he starts. He makes the calculations in table 3.1, which show the value of $1,000 saved at ages 20, 30, 40, and 50, assuming he retires at age 65 and can realize 10 percent per year from investment returns.

Example outside discipline: Bacteria are tiny but multiply quickly—in hospitable environments, they can double every thirty minutes. That means that after a day you would have 2.8×10^{14} bacteria, and after a week you would have over a googol (10^{100}) of bacteria. Exponential growth can lead to some truly mind-blowing results! This only holds true if the bacteria have enough to eat, though, which they certainly will not, as there are only 10^{80} atoms in the known universe, and not all of them are edible!

Discussion: Understanding compound interest from a financial perspective is important, as it allows you to forecast bank balances and other investments when making budgets and other projections. However, the concepts of compound interest and exponential growth—that there can be a substantial multiplier effect over time—are broadly applicable to concepts such as one's reputation, learning, and health. Small increases, over time, can compound or accumulate into large improvements—which means that it is worth seeking out consistent, gradual advances.

Sadly, this can work against you as well. If you borrow money, and are unable to repay the principal, then you will be paying interest on the initial amount as well as the previously charged interest. This is why credit card debt can be so pernicious, and many find themselves in ever-deepening holes.

The inverse of compound interest is "the time value of money." At a 10 percent interest rate, $100 in two years will become $121 ($100 × 110 percent × 110 percent, with interest compounded annually). Therefore, in exchange for being paid $121 in two years, you would accept $100 today (if you could invest it at 10 percent and arrive at the same outcome). The financial principle here is that the sooner you receive money, the more valuable it is. The more general principle is that time has value, as it gives you the freedom and optionality to invest both with your money and in your personal development.

The opposite of growth is decay, such as how children forget what they learned during the school year over the summer vacation. Fortunately, exponential decay means that you are losing a smaller amount each year, as the same percent decline is applied to a smaller base. Still, it is worth remembering that any knowledge base will have a natural rate of decay that you will have to actively offset if you want to maintain it. If you studied a language in high school but have not been regularly speaking it since then, you will know what I mean!

A related observation is the importance of protecting capital from losses. Investment examples frequently assume steady and continuous growth. However, in the real world there is always the chance of a large, negative event—a total wipeout. If this occurs, then the math dictates that any number times zero equals zero, no matter how high the returns were before or after that. Similarly, if you spend all your days living a law-abiding and moral life, but commit one heinous crime, your legacy will be one of dishonor and infamy. Protect both your financial and reputational capital well!

Exercises:

1. How much is $100 worth in ten years if it is invested at an annual interest rate of 12 percent?
2. At the peak of the internet bubble in the year 2000, investors believed that the future annual return of the stock market would be 30 percent, extrapolating the rate of appreciation from the previous five years. Why were these expectations unlikely to be accurate?
3. How is learning similar to compound interest?

CHECKLISTS

Discipline: Medicine

Summary: The human mind is incredibly capable in certain regards, but it falls short when performing some basic tasks. One of these challenges is keeping track of numerous objects, actions, or routines; having a written list thus makes a measurable difference with outcomes.

Why it is important: Checklists are a simple but powerful tool that compensate for an inherent weakness of the human mind. They are also a reminder that external tools can significantly aid our mental performance.

Example in discipline: Surgery is a complicated task but is comprised of basic steps—assembling the correct instruments, making incisions in the correct order, and so on. Many errors that are made during surgical procedures are not the result of a lack of skill but rather are simple, avoidable mistakes. When checklists are introduced into the operating room, these errors are much less common.

Example outside discipline: Pilots have checklists that they go through before each flight, investment analysts use them to ensure that various financial metrics are considered, and many people use "to do" lists regularly to make sure they don't forget routine tasks.

Discussion: It is important to remind ourselves that our brains are excellent at performing certain functions and poor at doing others. Conveniently, most of the tasks that the human brain finds challenging are performed well by computers—calculations, complex lists, and repetitive actions. It is far easier to rely on checklists—either on paper, electronic notes, or a dedicated program/app—than to attempt to maintain a complex list of events or procedures in your head.

Interestingly, it appears that the most common barriers to the adoption of checklists are pride and the belief that using a checklist is an admission of weakness. You might believe that your job requires so much skill that a simple checklist couldn't possibly help. But remember, if fighter jet pilots and surgeons need checklists, after spending decades training for and performing one specific activity, there is no shame in using a checklist when navigating the complexities of modern life.

In *The Checklist Manifesto* by Atul Gawande, the author focuses on the benefits that checklists bring to various fields, including medicine, business, construction, and law enforcement. Charlie Munger is a strong advocate of checklists in the investment field. And there are multi-billion-dollar companies whose workflow management software packages are basically just very fancy checklists!

Exercises:

1. Name some common everyday checklists that people use.
2. How are checklists complementary to Occam's razor?
3. Other than having a piece of paper handy, what are some ways to remember checklists?

REDUNDANCY

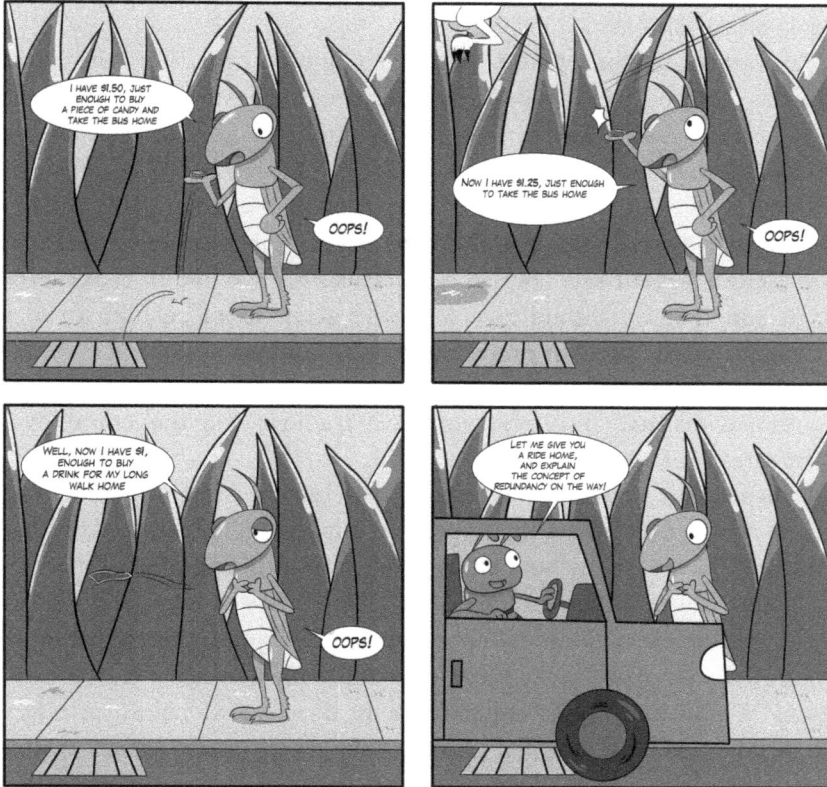

Discipline: Engineering

Summary: Engineers design bridges, cars, and medical implants to be as safe as possible, subject to constraints such as size, cost, and efficiency. To do this, they calculate the potential stresses, pressures, and other tolerances and then make sure that the materials and design are strong enough to withstand these forces. Finally, they add a little cushion to be extra safe, or perhaps in case they overlooked something. This is what we call *redundancy*, or margin of safety, and it prevents a disastrous outcome in case of unforeseen events.

Why it is important: Life is not predictable, so it is important to plan for some negative developments, especially when the consequences of failure are significant.

Example in discipline: A bridge is expected to support a maximum of twenty trucks at a time, each weighing 20,000 pounds. However, it is engineered to carry one hundred trucks so that it will not collapse even under the worst conditions.

Example outside discipline: You are going on a hike on a hot day and estimate that you will drink thirty-two ounces of water. You bring sixty-four ounces instead, just in case you get lost, the weather is especially warm, or a friend didn't bring enough.

Discussion: "Look both ways before crossing the street," "It's better to be safe than sorry," and "An ounce of prevention is worth a pound of cure." These are all sayings that remind us that we live in a dangerous world and that we should give ourselves some extra cushion to make it through safely. We can predict potential outcomes, but we must also plan for the outcomes that we don't expect—we must anticipate not only the rainstorms that come every year, but the hurricane that comes every fifty years.

With enough time and forethought, the human mind can understand various risks and calculate their potential impacts on the physical or financial world. There are the "known knowns," such as the number of trucks on the bridge, and the "known unknowns" like a massive hurricane that will strike roughly every decade. Our minds are less good at anticipating the "unknown unknowns,"[5] which could have equally damaging effects (Alien attack? Wind vortex?[6]). To compensate for these additional uncertainties, it is prudent to have a buffer, called a "margin of safety," which protects us in a disaster scenario. This concept is very popular in the investment world, where practitioners such as Warren Buffett and Seth Klarman employ it to mitigate the risk of capital loss should their investment theses prove incorrect.

On a related note, it is best to have several alternatives in case one of those options fails. This is true for problem-solving, and it is true for life. If you have trained for years to be a professional tennis player and then you break your arm badly, your future options are significantly limited. Therefore, wherever possible, redundancy should be incorporated into your career plans. While frequently this redundancy will end up being "wasted," since it is (by definition) only used on occasion, it should be viewed as a valuable contributor to lower stress levels, flexibility, negotiating leverage, and overall happiness. Just as many people will never collect a penny from their fire insurance (since most homes do not burn down), they still can sleep soundly knowing that they are protected from this catastrophic risk.

Exercises:

1. You are packing for a backpacking trip. You want to pack as lightly as possible but still be prepared for any type of weather. How might you approach this problem?
2. You are designing a mission-critical data center for your company. Where do you locate it?
3. Most Americans don't have enough savings to cover an unexpected $500 expense. Why is this a problem?

FEEDBACK LOOPS

Discipline: Biology

Summary: Certain systems, including those within living organisms and societies, adjust and respond automatically to changes. This can be a positively reinforcing action (where more of an output will trigger increased activity) or a negative one (more of the output triggers decreased activity).

Why it is important: Feedback loops are common and sometimes have negative consequences. By recognizing their presence, you will be able to lean into them if they are beneficial or stop them from escalating if they are not.

Example in discipline: The temperature of the human body needs to be maintained at around 99°F. If the temperature exceeds this, the brain prompts the release of sweat to cool the body down. If it drops too low, the brain increases body metabolism and shunts blood to its interior.

Example outside discipline: The increased temperature of the earth's surface due to global warming is leading to the accelerated melting of arctic ice. Since ice reflects sunlight (instead of absorbing solar energy as water does), when it melts, more energy is absorbed, and the earth warms even more quickly. The more ice that melts, the faster that global warming will occur; the higher the temperatures go, the more quickly the remaining ice will melt.

Discussion: When you get a good performance review at your job, you might get some financial reward, and generally your bosses and coworkers make you feel very good about yourself. This encourages you to work a little more and try a bit harder. As a result, your strong performance will continue into the next year, and might even improve. This is a very basic positive feedback loop, as the feedback pushes your behavior further in the same direction.

In a negative feedback loop, the outputs of a process will slow it down. A common example is when a business captures literal "negative feedback" from customer or employee surveys and uses those comments to improve its operating practices. Or when the price of something increases and impacts customer demand for it, such that it is optimal to reverse the price increase to maximize total profits.

It is important to distinguish between when an action is isolated and independent, and when it has consequences or repercussions (also referred to as "second-order effects"). Most of the time, when an action is taken, there is no further consequence—someone eats a banana, and that's the end of the story.[7] However, certain actions can set other reactions into effect that will either moderate or amplify these actions. In biology, these "feedback loops" are designed to keep the human body in balance (at the correct temperature, pH level, etc.). Feedback loops happen all the time in human interactions as well—if you are angry, you might yell, which makes someone else angry. Their yelling then increases your stress level, and the argument escalates. Or, you might make a mistake in front of other people, which causes you to blush. This physical reaction embarrasses you further, causes you to make more mistakes, and leads to further reddening.

If there are feedback loops present in a process, you should understand where they are so that you can take the appropriate action to stop them if the outcome is not what you desire. Similarly, if you can create a feedback loop that benefits you, it can lead to a desirable outcome. In the book *From Good to Great*, Jim Collins talks about the flywheel effect, where a business builds momentum and growth becomes largely self-propagating. This is a form of positive feedback loop, where the success of the business creates positive publicity and awareness from customers and partners, and this drives further growth.

Exercises:

1. There is something in basketball called the "hot hand" phenomenon, where players are thought to be prone to streaks of good and bad shooting. The evidence behind this is mixed, but if true, how could you explain this as a feedback loop? If not true, how could you explain that, also as a feedback loop?

2. Which of these is an example of a beneficial feedback loop?

   a. You exercise and get a lot of compliments on how healthy you look, so you feel like exercising more.
   b. You find a wallet, return it, and are given a small reward.
   c. You feed your dog from the table, so he keeps begging for food at the table.

3. You are a soccer coach, attempting to get your players to practice juggling the ball. How can you start a positive feedback loop to encourage this?

ACTIVATION ENERGY

ACTIVATION ENERGY

Discipline: Chemistry

Summary: A chemical reaction may be self-sustaining but still require a burst of energy to begin.

Why it is important: In science and in life, there are situations where a reaction "should" proceed—all the elements are in place. Yet it still needs some spark or external impetus to begin the process, after which it will propagate on its own.

Example in discipline: If you have a mixture of magnesium and oxygen, it will burn incredibly well until all the elements are consumed. But the reaction will not start until at least part of the magnesium is heated to 473°F. The energy required to start the reaction is called the activation energy.

Example outside discipline: Sam really likes playing soccer. But when he is lying on the couch, he has trouble finding the motivation to put on his shorts and cleats. It takes a little push to get him off the couch and ready to play, after which he can happily play soccer for many hours.

Discussion: Even when an outcome is desired, people, animals and processes need a little nudge to start. Much like the concept of inertia, there is a natural tendency to stay in a resting state unless forced to come out of it. Like a soapbox racer that needs a push to start down the hill (after which gravity will take over), sometimes people also need a little push.

Using some terminology from chemistry, an exothermic reaction (which releases energy) should happen spontaneously but usually does not. This is why wood doesn't just burst into flame, though once a part of it is on fire the rest will likely burn (the reaction is self-sustaining). The wood requires an activation energy to begin the reaction.[8]

A similar dynamic happens with a group of strangers attempting to engage in meaningful dialogue. It is difficult to start a conversation—there is some social awkwardness, and a good topic of conversation needs to be found. However, once the conversation is started, it frequently flows smoothly. This activation energy of meeting new people can hinder satisfying social connections from being made, so it is usually worthwhile to attempt to get over the proverbial hump.

In the business world, activation energy could take the form of persuading a customer to try a new product, writing the first lines of a code of a complex new project, or beginning to instill better habits (as James Clear discusses at length in *Atomic Habits*[9]). "The first step is the hardest," or something to that effect, because it involves motivation, risk, and change, and human beings have a hard time with all of those.

To convince people to take that first step, it is best to make it as easy as possible for them. In biology, an enzyme is a type of molecule that serves as a catalyst—it reduces the necessary activation energy and thus allows the reaction to occur more readily (figure 3.1). In the human interaction described above, a catalyst might be an ice-breaking game, some background music, or sharing a meal. For a business, a catalyst might be a free coupon, a limited-time offer, or some other carefully designed incentive system.

Exercises:

1. Your chemistry teacher explains to you that in order to start a certain reaction, you either need to provide the activation energy (by heating the reactants up to 200°F) or reduce the activation energy by adding a catalyst (in which case you would only need to heat to 125°F). Which is better?
2. You love playing beach volleyball but are having a hard time motivating yourself to stop watching Netflix and drive to the beach. What are some techniques you can use to lower your "activation energy"?
3. Is caffeine a useful way to lower the activation energy of beginning your day?

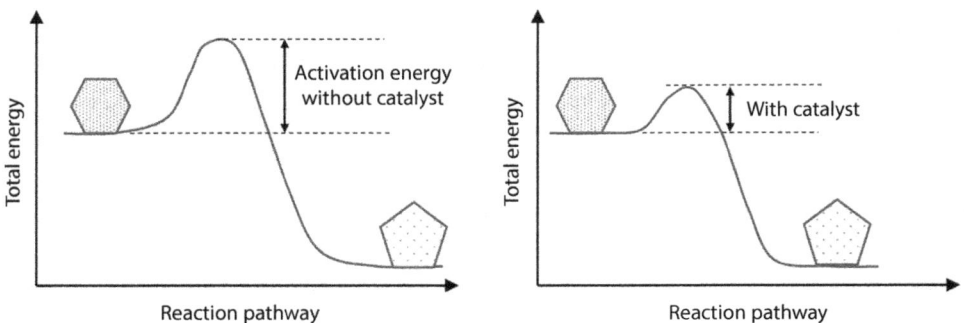

FIGURE 3.1 Activation energy with and without a catalyst.

DECISION VERSUS OUTCOME

Good Decision/Bad Outcome and Bad Decision/Good Outcome

Discipline: Medicine

Summary: Just because something turns out well doesn't mean it was a good decision, and vice versa.

Why it is important: Separating the decision-making process from the observed outcome is of paramount importance. We can control the decision and gather information to make better decisions, but the outcome is never totally predictable. Focusing on improving our decision-making process will frequently lead to good results, but not always, and we must not let those chance disappointments negatively impact us.

Example in discipline: After a complicated pregnancy, the baby is at risk during labor. Despite this, the doctor decides to deliver the baby vaginally instead of surgically (via a Caesarean section). The baby is born healthy, but as the doctor reviews his vital signs, she realizes that the delivery was a lot riskier than she had initially thought and had only a 10 percent chance of being free of complications. She had made a bad decision but lucked into a good outcome. Down the hall there is an uncomplicated pregnancy, and the doctor makes the easy choice to deliver the baby vaginally. This time, an unlikely complication (which only happens 1 percent of the time) led to a distressed newborn. This is an example of a good decision with a bad outcome.

Example outside discipline: You take your car to the mechanic and are told that the brakes should be replaced, as they have a 25 percent chance of total failure at highway speeds. Since you are short on money, you decide to risk it and drive across country to visit your friends. Luckily, the brakes hold up.

Discussion: Sometimes you do something that is dumb, but it turns out okay. And sometimes you make a great decision, and it still turns out badly. It is important to focus on making the best decisions possible, since frequently only the decision (not the outcome) is in your control. The better the decision-making process, the more beneficial outcomes will result, even though some of the outcomes will still be negative.

Even the best decisions carry with them the probability of bad outcomes, but knowing this does not mean that you should do anything differently. The *ex-ante* (what is known before the event occurs) probability is the only measure on which you can rely, since the *ex-post* (what happened) information isn't available at the time. Making an even-odds wager where you win 99 times out of 100 is a very good bet, but 1/100 of the time you will still lose the bet. Similarly, making an even-odds bet where you only win 1/100 times is a very bad bet, but occasionally you will still win. The outcome that transpires doesn't change the soundness of the original decision to make the bet.

Importantly, focusing on the decision itself and the procedure used to arrive at that decision allows you to improve your process and make better decisions over time. You generally can't do this by looking at outcomes, since you don't usually have enough information to draw meaningful conclusions. In a business setting, you may have some data (doing A/B testing for a website promotion, for example), but in a personal setting, many decisions are only made once. So, pay attention to the inputs and the process of the decision, and then accept the results, whatever they may be!

Exercises:

1. Characterize these situations as good or bad decisions, with good or bad outcomes:

   a. You throw a knife in the air and catch it by its handle.

   b. You go to a Las Vegas casino and play the wheel of fortune. You win $100.

   c. You eat healthily and exercise regularly. Still, you contract a rare virus and are sick for a month.

   d. You drink alcohol and drive a car. You get into an accident and total the car.

   e. You pet a dog without asking first if it is friendly, but it doesn't bite you.

2. Your friend is bragging to you about how he didn't study for a math test, which ended up being canceled due to the teacher getting sick. How do you respond?

3. You do a lot of research on buying a new phone. You buy the phone that you think is the best phone for a reasonable price. One month after buying it, the manufacturer recalls it, saying that the battery may catch on fire. How would you describe this?

LEVERAGE

LEVERAGE

Discipline: Physics/engineering

Summary: Leverage refers to the ability to get more results out of a smaller amount of force or work. A lever is a mechanical device, but the concept is also relevant in financial, personal, and work contexts.

Why it is important: The ability to get greater results from the same amount of effort is attractive in a variety of different areas. Using physical, financial, or psychological levers can be a powerful approach to solving problems.

Example in discipline: A crowbar is an example of a basic lever. Using one, it is quite easy to lift an object as heavy as a refrigerator, which would be very difficult to move without any tools.

Example outside discipline: Financial leverage allows you to make (or lose) a large amount of money. An investment that might return 10 percent without leverage could easily be leveraged to make or lose 100 percent based on the same fundamental outcomes.[10]

Discussion: Leverage, in a sense, is amplification and power. You can lift more weight with the appropriate lever or pulley system (figure 3.2),[11] you can earn more money if you use debt in your financial structure, and you can accrue larger professional gains if you have leverage to use on coworkers, customers, or suppliers. This brings with it a sense of power, as those with the most leverage will frequently bring the greatest force to bear in each situation and thus be positioned to dictate what occurs.

FIGURE 3.2 Leverage in the literal, physical sense. https://pixabay.com/vectors/archimedes-lever-quarryman-worker-148273/.

Leverage is both good and bad. In the physical realm, where the use of tools allows humans to accomplish greater tasks,[12] it is generally good. In the financial world, too much debt (a type of leverage) has frequently led to financial ruin. More abstractly, though, leverage is a type of influence that can be used for both good and evil (e.g., blackmail is a type of leverage).

If it is possible to do more with less, then it is generally desirable to do so. However, the downside of this approach should also be kept in mind—the *margin of safety* can be quite thin. Ideally, you should look for situations that allow you to "leverage" existing knowledge, connections, or infrastructure to achieve a beneficial outcome with less effort.

One popular example of leverage (in my nerdy circles, at least) is the Pareto principle or 80/20 rule, which states that 20 percent of inputs (causes) lead to 80 percent of outputs (effects). Stated differently, 20 percent of effort leads to 80 percent of the results. Naturally, to enjoy the greatest improvement from a given amount of effort, you should focus on doing more of this 20 percent! As a business, this could be your most popular products, best customers, or most productive employees. As a person, it could be the activities that bring you the most pleasure, make you the most money, or help you lead the healthiest lifestyle. Figure out what matters the most, and then do more of it!

Exercises:

1. Which of these devices provides physical leverage: the wheelbarrow, bottle opener, pulley, shovel, or sponge?
2. You purchase a home for $1 million. You put $200,000 down and borrow $800,000 using a mortgage. You sell the home ten years later for $2 million. Ignoring interest costs and taxes, what is your profit percentage compared to the home price, and what is the profit percentage on your investment (the $200,000 down payment, also known as equity)?
3. You run a company that supplies food to local restaurants. A friend has a company that is hoping to supply beverages to the same restaurants. Can you think of an example of potential leverage here?

4

Economics and Business

Economics may seem like a dry and boring field, and in some cases, it is.[1] But at its core, economics (and especially the subfield of microeconomics) is the study of what causes people to make decisions—the motivations, incentives, and criteria that influence them. This is important information, especially since you are not always conscious of these influences, even when they play a large role in your life. For instance, do you really, truly know what motivates you? Is it success, money, the respect of your friends, fear and/or love of your parents, power, or something else? And even if you do know exactly *what* it is that drives you, do you know *why* this is the case? If you are going to work your butt off to climb up the corporate ranks and become a partner, shouldn't you figure out now, instead of in twenty years, whether the foundation of your motivation is solid enough to get you through the challenging path ahead?

Academic research into businesses has been a fertile area for the examination of decisions and their consequences. Business is also at the intersection of money and human relationships, and for obvious reasons these are both areas in which people should really strive to make the best decisions they can. As a result, there are many concepts from the business world that are applicable to life more broadly, especially with regard to the interactions you will have with others in both cooperative and adversarial situations.

SUNK COST

SUNK COST

Discipline: Economics

Summary: A sunk cost is a resource (money, time, health, etc.) that has already been spent, is unrecoverable, and thus shouldn't be factored into future decisions.

Why it is important: Making good decisions requires understanding which information to utilize and which to disregard. Using irrelevant or misleading data will lead you to make suboptimal decisions; hence, sunk costs should be consciously ignored.

Example in discipline: Sara spends $100 on a nonrefundable bus ticket to visit her friend. She is then offered a free plane ticket to make the same trip. While she regrets spending the $100, she realizes that she is still better off taking the plane than the bus.

Example outside discipline: The extended U.S. involvement in Vietnam was at least partially due to the sunk cost fallacy. After a decade of fighting, so many American lives, as well as economic and political capital, had been lost that it was very difficult to abandon the war effort, despite the increasingly poor prospects for victory.

Discussion: Making good decisions is an important life skill that we will discuss in detail later in this book. As discussed in chapter 1, there are mental shortcuts and misconceptions that prevent us from making optimal decisions even when we have enough information to do so. One natural tendency is to form attachments, or "anchors," which are great for strengthening human relationships but less good when the attachment is to inanimate objects that would best be let go. Put differently, an anchor can be helpful during a bad storm, but it can also drag you down to the bottom of the ocean, which would kind of suck. So, avoid unintentional anchors!

After we make decisions, we are emotionally committed to those decisions, at least partially because we don't want to admit we are wrong. A sunk cost is a painful reminder of a mistake we made—where we wasted time, money, or effort. But since it is (by definition) something that cannot be changed, the best that we can do is to make better decisions going forward. A $90 loss is better than a $100 loss, and crying over spilled milk won't change that. Have you ever cried over spilled milk? It seems like all those tears would just make it even messier to clean up . . . so don't do it!

Corollary: Opportunity Costs

Sunk costs are *explicit* outlays that *should not* be considered when assessing future options. In contrast, opportunity costs are *hidden* costs that *should* be considered. Specifically, an opportunity cost is the foregone income or experience that will not be enjoyed should a certain path be chosen. The cost of traveling the world for a year is not just the expense of plane tickets and hotels, but also the foregone savings and work experience you would have accumulated if you had stayed at your job. The benefit of spending an hour finding the best coupon code for a purchase may be the $10 savings from the website, but the opportunity cost of that hour can be measured in money (how much money could you have made working for that hour) or pleasure (could you have exercised or read a book instead?)

Opportunity costs remind us that life does not exist in a vacuum. Decisions are made on a regular basis that require trade-offs and sacrifices, and it is best to acknowledge these explicitly. Money is the easiest metric to measure this cost, as it is fungible—it is clear from your bank account balance that if you spend $500 on a dinner, those savings are no longer available to buy a PlayStation 5. Other costs are less obvious— leisure time, career achievement, the strength of relationships, physical health, and sleep are all areas where opportunity costs should be considered.

Exercises:

1. You buy two tickets to a concert. A friend calls you that afternoon and offers you free tickets to a different show that is happening at the same time. You would prefer to see the second show. Should you still go to the first concert?
2. You order too much food at a restaurant and are full after you have eaten only half of it. You have always been taught to finish what is on your plate. Should you finish the food?
3. You start writing a final paper on the topic of SPAC investment successes. After ten hours of work, you realize that your topic was a poor choice due to lack of supporting evidence and that you should probably switch if you want to get an A. What do you do?

EXPECTED VALUE

EXPECTED VALUE

Panel 1: I'M SAVING SO MUCH MONEY ON PARKING. I FIGURED OUT THAT I ONLY HAVE A 10% CHANCE OF GETTING A TICKET, WHICH COSTS ME $50

Panel 2: I SEE. SO YOUR EXPECTED COST IS 10% X $50, OR ONLY $5. A GARAGE COSTS $20, SO YOU SHOULD TAKE THE RISK GETTING THE TICKET

Panel 3: EXACTLY! PARKING ILLEGALLY HAS A VERY POSITIVE EXPECTED VALUE

Panel 4: YOUR EXPECTED VALUE WILL BE LOWER AFTER THE TOWING FEE. HOW MANY UNPAID PARKING TICKETS DO YOU HAVE?

Discipline: Economics

Summary: Expected value is the sum of values of all potential outcomes, with the magnitude of each outcome weighted by the chance of that outcome occurring.

Why it is important: Expected value combines the *probabilities* of events occurring with the *importance* or *values* of those events. Knowing either of these variables alone is insufficient, but both together give you a powerful decision-making tool.

Example in discipline: In a gambling game based on flipping a coin, you are paid $1 if you flip a head but nothing if you flip a tail. The expected value of each flip is calculated as 50% × $1 + 50% × $0, which equals $.50.

Example outside discipline: Ted goes to a carnival and decides to play the ring toss. He estimates that he has a 1 percent chance of getting a ring on a bottle, in which case he will win a $10 stuffed animal. Each toss costs $1, so he realizes that the expected value of each toss is 1% × $10 + 99% × $0, or $.10 – $1, which is –$.90.

Discussion: Let's say I ask you to play a game with the following rules: I flip a coin, and if it lands as heads you get $2, but if it lands as tails, you lose $1. You will have to pay me a quarter each time you flip the coin, though. Should you play?

Well, per figure 4.1, half the time (when you flip heads), you will win $2, so your expected value from flipping heads = (probability of flipping heads) × (what you get if you flip heads) = ½ × $2, or $1. Half the time you will lose $1, so your expected value from flipping tails = ½ × (–$1), or –$.50. Your total expected value from each flip of the coin is the sum of these outcomes, or $.50 ($1 – $.50), which is more than the cost of the game ($.25). If you played this game over and over, you would expect to

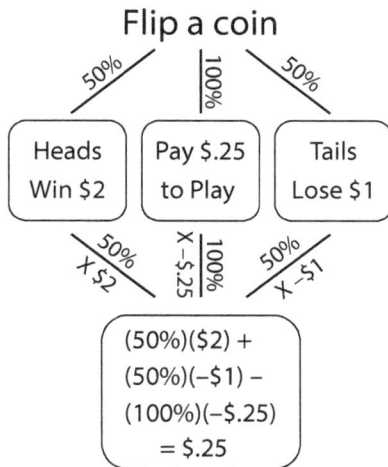

FIGURE 4.1 The expected value of a coin flip game.

win around $.25 each time you flipped the coin, which would add up after a few hundred flips!

Now, what if I tell you that I have been tricking you and that the coin isn't a real coin, but rather a fake coin that I had borrowed from a magician. Instead of landing on heads half the time, it only lands on heads ¼ of the time, and tails ¾ of the time. Should you play the game?

Doing the same calculations, you now expect to win $2 only ¼ of the time, with an expected value of ¼ × $2, or $.50. Three-fourths of the time, you now expect to lose $1, so ¾ × (–$1) or –$.75 is the expected value of flipping tails. Your total expected value is now –$.25, which means that you will lose a quarter (on average) each time you flip the coin, even before you paid the $.25 to play. Knowing about expected value has saved you from playing a sure money loser!

Even with an unfair coin, it could still be a profitable game to play if the prize were very large when heads did come up. For example, let's say you could win $100 when heads came up. You'd be more than happy to play that game, because when you won, you would win a lot more than you lost.

Expected value can be applied to analyzing whether to buy a lottery ticket (a one in a million chance to win $500,000 is a bad bet) and which career path to follow (should you join your mother's firm or pursue your dream of being a stand-up comedian?). It also works for negative expected values (in other words, expected losses)—if there is a 1 percent chance of getting a $50 parking ticket, then it is an acceptable risk to park illegally ($.50 expected loss), but if there is a 1 percent chance of dying after cliff diving, then it is a terrible idea (1 percent of an infinite loss is still infinite).

Expected value is closely related to many concepts in different fields:

1. Severity and incidence from the world of insurance—how much an accident will cost to remedy (called "severity," e.g., the expense of fixing your car after an accident) multiplied by the likelihood of this scenario (called "incidence" or "frequency," i.e., the chance of getting into a bad crash).
2. For sports fans out there, it is like a slugging percentage in baseball—the chance of getting on base (batting average) weighted by how many bases you usually advance when you do get a hit.

3. Finance geeks will be pleased to know that expected value is an integral part of all options pricing approaches, including the Black-Scholes model.

4. The concept of "pot odds" in poker is also an expected value calculation—the decision to stay in the hand depends both on your chance of winning the hand and the size of the pot relative to the necessary bet. For instance, if you estimate that you only have a 10 percent chance of winning a poker hand, but the final bet is just 5 percent of the total pot amount, then you should throw in those chips—the expected value is positive.

In so many fields, knowing either the chance or the magnitude of an event isn't sufficient, but both together will provide a solid basis on which to make decisions. To shamelessly repeat myself, expected value is an important concept because it considers both the *probabilities* of different outcomes and the *value* of those outcomes when they happen. You should try to play games (and pursue life situations) with high likelihoods of *good* outcomes or low likelihoods of *great* outcomes. Conversely, you should avoid areas that provide high likelihoods of *bad* outcomes or low likelihoods of *terrible* outcomes.

Exercises:

1. What is the expected value of a lottery ticket where you have a one in a million chance of winning the $500,000 prize and it costs $1?

2. You can buy or lease a car. If you buy it, the car costs $50,000. If you lease it, the lease payments are a total of $20,000 over 3 years, at which point you can buy the car for $35,000. You think that there is a 50 percent chance that you will end up purchasing the car after the lease period. What is the expected cost of the lease versus purchasing it?

3. You estimate that by going 80 mph instead of 60 mph, your fuel mileage decreases from 20 mpg to 15 mpg. Additionally, you have a 5 percent chance of getting a speeding ticket, which costs $200. You are taking a 240-mile trip. How much time will you save, and how much extra will it cost, if you go 80 mph and gas costs $3/gallon?

INCENTIVES

Discipline: Business/economics

Summary: Incentives are the positive or negative rewards that are meant to influence certain behaviors or outcomes.

Why it is important: Humans respond to economic and noneconomic incentives when deciding how to act. Altering incentives can have a significant impact on decisions and outcomes.

Example in discipline: A corporate manager will be paid $1 million if he is able to increase revenues by 20 percent. He runs an aggressive discounting program to increase sales 20 percent and get his bonus, but the company earns less money as a result since the discounts were so large. The incentive here was set improperly, and the manager responded to it in a way that was optimal for him but not for the company.

Example outside discipline: Your child hasn't been doing well at school. You tell her that she can get out of a week's worth of chores if she gets an

A on her next test. She studies hard and gets a perfect score, calculating that the time she spent studying was less painful than the time she would have to spend on her chores.

Discussion: Incentives in life can be tangible (e.g., money) or emotional (e.g., parental approval), extrinsic or intrinsic, explicitly stated or merely implied. Humans respond to incentives whether they know it or not, and other people and businesses intentionally shape incentives to drive the behaviors they desire. A collection of incentives is called an "incentive structure," and these structures exist all around us—at school, at home, on the playground, and in the workplace. It is important to know your own motivations and from where your internal and external incentives derive.

It is also important to understand why others are giving you certain incentives and what they gain by doing so. If a company offers you a coupon for $1 off two boxes of cereal, their motivation is obvious—they want you to buy more cereal. Other incentives are not as clear or benign—an online gambling platform that offers a "risk-free" bet forces you to keep betting on the platform to try to recoup your losses, increasing the chances that you grow addicted to the activity.

Everyone is motivated by a different combination of factors (money, power, guilt, parental approval, love, achievement, and fear, to name a few), and shaping incentives to match the person can lead to better outcomes for everyone. That said, it is also important to understand that poorly constructed incentives can lead to bad outcomes. For instance, surgeons are paid well if they operate and thus are likely to have a financial incentive to recommend a surgical solution to a medical problem. As the lucky recipient of several unnecessary (in hindsight) surgeries, I have some first-hand experiences with this, and I don't recommend it!

Inverting the concept of incentives, consider cui bono, the legal principle that states that those who derive the greatest benefit from committing a crime are the most likely to be guilty. When examining an outcome and attempting to understand how it came to pass, remember to examine the incentives of all parties involved.

Exercises:

1. You want your son to clean his room. To get him to do this, you offer to double his allowance if he cleans his room when it gets particularly messy. Is this a good idea?

2. You want your daughter to do more volunteer work. You promise her that if she spends one hundred hours volunteering, she can get a new phone. Is this a good idea?
3. A company wants to reward its workers by paying them overtime for every hour they work beyond forty hours per week. It also wants them to have the flexibility to choose whatever hours they want to work. What is a potential unintended consequence of this scheme?

DECLINING MARGINAL UTILITY

DECLINING MARGINAL BENEFIT

Discipline: Economics

Summary: The benefit derived from any object or activity declines as its quantity increases, until it approaches zero.

Why it is important: It is simpler to think in linear terms, but our brains' perceptions of the world are not, in fact, linear. Preferences, benefits, and enjoyment usually proceed on a curved or asymptotic path, and knowing the shape of this path helps us to make good decisions about the future.

Example in discipline: Adding a certain machine to a factory floor increases production by 100 percent. Adding a second machine increases production by only 50 percent more, since most of the difficult work is already being done by the first machine. Adding a third machine doesn't increase production at all, since there are no tasks remaining for which the third machine can be used.

Example outside discipline: A friend of yours has never tried chocolate, as his parents tricked him and told him he was allergic when he was a child.[2] He has his first bite and loves it. Then he has another, and another. By his twentieth piece of chocolate, he starts feeling sick, and each bite he takes after that provides a negative benefit, until he never wants to eat chocolate again!

Discussion: The human mind will adjust to almost anything. So, when you first try a new flavor of bubble tea, you might love it and think you will never tire of it. But inevitably, the more that you drink, the less special it tastes, until you get sick just thinking about those tapioca pearls. This holds true for food, possessions, and even experiences—the first ones are great, the next few are only pretty good, and at some point, you have just had too many.

In economics, this concept is known as declining marginal benefit or declining marginal utility, which means that each additional ("marginal") object or experience provides slightly less pleasure or benefit than the one before it. It also applies to drugs (known as "habituation" or "building tolerance"), so that not only does your body crave a drug after you have first taken it, but you will need more of it each time to experience the same effect. Clearly, this is not a great situation in which to put yourself!

Fortunately, this applies in reverse to negative or difficult experiences— there is frequently a declining *marginal cost* for most unpleasant activities. The first day of exercising can be agonizing, but it gets easier as you get into the habit of repeating the task. Doing one load of laundry isn't fun, but doing two loads at one time is not twice as bad (especially since you can dry one load while you are washing the other). In general, extrapolating the pain or pleasure from your first experience will lead you to overestimate the total pain or pleasure from repeated experiences. This is because our brains act to adjust the pleasure and pain stimuli so that both diminish over time.

I will mention the Pareto principle (or 80/20 rule) again in this context. The top 20 percent of causes have the highest utility and therefore generate most of the results. As the marginal benefit declines, other causes generate increasingly fewer results. As before, the lesson here is simple: focus on the areas of life and work that provide the highest marginal utility, aka the most bang for the buck.[3]

Exercises:

1. You try a new ice cream flavor (chocolate salted caramel brownie swirl) and LOVE it. You are about to buy an entire five-gallon tub of it (the one they serve from at the ice cream store), when your friend reminds you of something. What did she tell you?
2. The iPhone 5 (and all previous versions) had a four-inch screen, while the iPhone 6 had a five-inch screen. Many people upgraded to the iPhone 6, but when the iPhone 7 was released, with a faster processor and better camera (but still a five-inch screen), sales results were disappointing. Why do you think that is?
3. A friend offers you a deal—he will cook spaghetti for one for $10, charge $15 for two people, and $20 for four. Why do you think he charges this way?

NEGOTIATIONS

Discipline: Business

Summary: In head-to-head negotiations, it is frequently possible for both parties to benefit. The way to ensure this happens is to find variables that are valued differently by the two parties, such as money, time, responsibility, or creative preferences.

Why it is important: Nearly every day brings a new business or personal negotiation, and you will have to make some compromises. The more of these outcomes that can be win/win, the better!

Example in discipline: Bob and Mary are negotiating Bob's salary. Bob wants a raise, but Mary doesn't have enough money to pay him much more. However, as they discuss it further, it turns out that Bob doesn't need the money now, he just feels under pressure to increase his retirement savings. So, Mary starts a retirement account for Bob that can be funded on a tax-advantaged basis over a much longer period.

Example outside discipline: You want to go shopping, but your brother wants to go to his friend's house, and you don't have time to do both. You discuss it further and realize that the reason your brother wants to go to his friend's house is to borrow his baseball mitt. You suggest bringing your old baseball mitt to the sporting goods store to have it fixed, so that your brother can use it.

Discussion: If I love ice cream and don't like candy, while my friend has the opposite preference, then we can trade ice cream for candy and both be better off. Negotiations can follow a similar path, but first you must figure out which variables are valued differently. For instance, I may dislike working on accounting spreadsheets but enjoy interacting with customers, while my coworker may have the opposite preference. If it is not possible to find outputs that are valued differently, though, then it is more difficult to negotiate, since it becomes a zero-sum game. This is when any benefit I receive is roughly equal to the loss that my negotiating partner must bear.

It is easy to assume that others want the same thing you do (be it money, power, candy, or something else) but people usually have different needs and desires. Instead of assuming that a certain situation is zero-sum, ask others what they really prefer, since you may find an outcome that benefits everyone. Also, zero-sum negotiations seem to end with at least one party (the worse negotiator) feeling aggrieved, which can damage personal relationships or workplace morale.

If you can't have a negotiation where everyone wins, then you also need to figure out who is in a stronger negotiating position. The way to do this is to understand who has the most to lose if no agreement can be reached. If you can just walk away from the negotiation with indifference, while your partner will be really upset (or economically damaged) if you don't come to some agreement, then you have more negotiating leverage. You can choose how aggressively to apply this leverage, of course.

It is important to understand your negotiating partner's best alternative,[4] since this will determine their willingness to reach an agreement. For instance, let's say your friend wants to borrow your bicycle, since his bike is broken. If this is the only way for him to get to his boyfriend's house, he may be willing to give up quite a lot to borrow the bike. On the other hand, if he has other options (take a bus, borrow a bike from someone else, or take a long walk) he will probably refuse to negotiate if your demands are too large.

Exercises:

1. It is Halloween, and three friends have just finished trick or treating. Table 4.1 shows who likes which candy the best (each rating is 1 out of 10). Propose some trades that leave both parties better off.
2. You need a higher salary to pay a babysitter to pick up your children after school. Your boss is very reluctant to give you a raise, however, since the company is not doing that well. What might be a solution that works for both you and your boss?
3. A real estate developer has bought every house on your block except yours and is planning on tearing them all down to build a large condominium high rise. He has spent $50 million, and you calculate that he will likely make $100 million in profits from the development. He cannot start the project until he owns your property. At what price would you sell him your house?

Table 4.1 Candy relative preferences

	Juan	Madison	Quinn
Kit Kat	10	8	5
Mounds	2	8	9
Snickers	5	4	10

COMPARATIVE ADVANTAGE

Discipline: Business

Summary: Different countries, companies, and people have varying skills and abilities. It is economically advantageous to focus on the area in which you have the greatest opportunity to differentiate yourself from others.

Why it is important: Knowing one's circles of competence is important, but it is also necessary to understand that all strengths are relative. You should try to emphasize your best *relative* strengths in business and in life.

Example in discipline: A French farmer can choose to produce ten cases of wine or five pounds of cheese. A British farmer is not as productive and can make either two cases of wine or four pounds of cheese. Even though the French farmer can make both more wine and more cheese than the British one, she is still better off only making wine, since this is where her comparative advantage lies (5 times as productive instead of just 25 percent more). She can then trade some of her wine for British cheese and have more total consumption.

Example outside discipline: You are the founder of an internet company. You are an extremely talented and hard-working person, and it turns out that in addition to writing great computer code, you can also make coffee and submit expense reports more efficiently than your office manager. Still, you should spend all your time writing code, since this is where your greatest comparative advantage lies; let your office manager make the coffee.

Discussion: It is frustrating to be good at something and watch others do it badly. But it is usually optimal to do exactly this so that you can stay focused on areas in which you have a real advantage. This concept originated in discussions around trade,[5] where many nations decided it was best to focus on doing one activity particularly well and then used the products of that industry to trade for other desired goods. However, it is equally applicable to basic human interactions and activities.

The profession in which you are likely to be most successful is not the one where you are the best on an absolute basis, but rather the one where you have the greatest performance differential versus your competition. In the land of the blind, the one-eyed man is king, even if that same man may not do so well against two-eyed competitors! So, if you are studying big data analytics and so is everyone else in the Ivy League, you may have trouble getting a plum job. But, if you are getting a PhD in sheep husbandry, your competition will likely be slightly less intense. That career decision might not be such a baaaaaahd idea after all.

Exercises:

1. You are a freelance copywriter and get paid $100/hour (after taxes) for your work. You can work as much as you like, and you enjoy your work (lucky you!). You are considering hiring someone to clean your house, since you dislike cleaning toilets. He charges $50 an hour, which seems like a lot to pay for a toilet cleaner. Do you hire him anyway?

2. Toby loves playing soccer and can play any position. He is best at midfield, but the team has three players who are better at that position. He is also a decent goalie, and since no one else can really play goalie, this is where he is usually placed. Is this a good outcome?
3. If there is a trend of families with high-school–aged children moving out of New York City to sparsely populated states such as South Dakota, having them learn the oboe and quit baseball to take up fencing, what might explain it?

GAME THEORY AND DEDUCTIVE REASONING

GAME THEORY AND DEDUCTIVE REASONING

Discipline: Economics

Summary: It is frequently possible to predict how a given situation will resolve itself if you know the motivations and therefore the likely actions of each of the parties involved.

Why it is important: Thinking one step ahead and understanding second-order effects are important aspects of making good decisions.

Example in discipline: Company A and B both bid for a project. The customer mistakenly sent an email marked "Confidential" from Company A to a member of Company B's team, which included their anticipated bid amount. Company B structured their bid to be slightly better than this amount but still lost the project to Company A, which realized what happened and thus bid a lower amount than was in the email.

Example outside discipline: You need to buy either lemonade (which goes well with sandwiches) or soda (which goes well with pizza) for a picnic. Your friend is buying the food, but his phone has died, so you can't ask what he chose. You realize that your friend is very considerate and knows how much you love pizza. Thus, you buy soda, anticipating this outcome.

Discussion: The process of making decisions, whether in personal or business settings, can be incredibly complex. Nonetheless, outcomes may be accurately anticipated based on economic or personal motivations and incentives.

An old example of deductive logic is that of three prisoners, lined up facing forward, such that each can see the colors of the hats on the heads of the men ahead of him but not his own. Each can use what they see in conjunction with others' silences to deduce each person's hat color.[6]

This is obviously a contrived example, but it is important to realize that even the most complex problems can usually be simplified by considering what others are or are not doing, and where their motivations lie. When Kennedy was facing down Khrushchev during the Cuban Missile Crisis, he could either remain passive or aggressively lobby for Russia to remove the missiles.[7] He enlisted the help of the Nobel Prize winning game theorist Thomas Shelling, who persuaded him to act swiftly, which ended up defusing the situation. Note that there currently exists a similar dynamic with a nuclearized North Korea; however, since we cannot assume that our "opponent" will act rationally in this case, game theory may prove less relevant.

Additionally, we must be careful to frame the situation correctly. If we don't, we might end up with suboptimal conclusions, such as:

- Nothing is better than eternal happiness.
- Something is better than nothing.
- Therefore, something is better than eternal happiness.

The most effective way to incorporate this concept into your life and decision-making processes is simply to think a few steps ahead. Don't be content to choose a course of action based on only the immediate outcomes (known as "first-order effects"). Consider the consequences of the action, what others might do in response to this action, and how the sequence of events will play out—"second-order effects." For example, say that your boss asks you to submit false accounting results for a regulatory filing, and you think it is unlikely that you will get caught; you consider acquiescing. However, you then consider second- and third-order effects: if you get away with it, he will likely ask again; he may ask others to do the same, and those people might report him to the authorities; he could blame the fraud on you. You decide that it would be a bad decision (even putting morality aside).

Finally, consider this real-world example of game theory, where Olympic badminton teams tried to lose their matches to secure favorable placement for the next round.[8] It was highly amusing watching the players intentionally miss shots, and the commentary was priceless. However, these players did not consider the second-order effects, which in this case meant the disqualification of both teams from the tournament!

Exercises:

1. Everyone closes their eyes and must raise either their right or left hand. If everyone raises their right hands, each participant will receive $10. If only one person raises her left hand, she will receive $500. If more than one person raises their left hand, no one receives any money. What do you predict will happen?

2. You are at a charity auction, bidding for a painting that you like. You bid $100, but someone else bids $150. You bid $200, but the same person bids $250. What can you do to ensure that you win the auction, at the lowest possible cost?

3. You are playing a game of chicken, where you and your rival are driving cars directly at each other at 100 mph. If you swerve, you must give your

rival your car. If she swerves, she must give her car to you. If neither of you swerves, you both die. What is your best course of action?

NETWORK EFFECTS AND ECONOMIES OF SCALE

Discipline: Business

Summary: Certain products or services become more valuable the more people that use them. Networks are formed from people using services and companies providing the services. The larger these networks get, the more benefits they provide to the customers and the cheaper they are to maintain. Therefore, more can be invested to make the service even better, and a virtuous cycle ensues.

Why it is important: Networks play a role in many facets of life, and their power is directly proportional to their size and number of connections. The power of networks extends to business, power dynamics, and personal relationships.

Example in discipline: Many people joined Facebook or Instagram, since with over 1 billion users, it is highly likely that your friends and family are on those networks already. With the money that Meta (both companies' corporate parent) earns selling advertising to its large user base, it can invest a significant amount to improve the services, making them faster, more highly featured, and more reliable.

Example outside discipline: As a teen, you frequented a certain pizza place after school, since most of your friends went there as well. One of the reasons it was popular was that the pizza was cheap, since the store could sell a lot of pizza and still profit from the high volume.

Discussion: Sometimes, bigger is indeed better. A larger network provides better results for all participants in the network, and the more users a network has, the more valuable it becomes. Economies of scale allow a large company to spend more dollars (on research and development, advertising, or a bigger factory) yet have these costs comprise a lower percentage of revenues, giving it a competitive advantage against a smaller company.

In extreme cases, these advantages can grow to be so large that the company becomes a monopoly or close to it. Amazon, for example, has the most online shopping customers, the most third-party sellers (companies that sell on Amazon's website and use Amazon's fulfillment operations), and the largest network of warehouses. Customers go to Amazon, since it has the best selection, the lowest prices, and the quickest delivery times. And the more customers that use Amazon, the more sellers will want to use Amazon as well; the larger Amazon becomes, the more warehouses they can build. Eventually, no other company will be able to compete with Amazon's cost or speed of delivery.

This does not have to be the case. Many businesses don't really benefit from getting larger, and in fact may grow too large for their own good. Frequently there are also regulatory measures that are implemented to stop this from happening. For example, in professional sports, the richest teams must share revenues with the poorest ones, since otherwise the teams from major cities (with wealthier fans and more lucrative television contracts) would always make the most money and could thus lure the best players. The large-market teams would then be more successful,[9] thereby allowing them to charge more for tickets and television rights, and the cycle would continue.

If you are starting a business, it is best to focus on an idea that will benefit from these economies of scale, as well as to try not to compete with a company that already enjoys them. Nvidia is a great business, as their graphics processors have significant technical advantages, but trying to compete against them at this point would be almost impossible.

You are likely intuitively aware of network effects already. For example, perhaps you chose to study Spanish instead of French, since there are many more native Spanish speakers with whom you can converse. You may have bought an iPhone, since there are so many more apps written for the iOS platform (developers write apps based on their potential revenues, which is determined by the number of customers and their propensity to spend), and your friends all prefer the blue text bubbles. And you probably use popular services like Amazon, Instagram, and Google almost every day.

Conversely, it is important to be aware of how network effects can lead to an undesirable outcome. You might want to support your small local businesses by accepting higher prices, knowing that they can't match Amazon's prices and survive economically. And you should understand that network effects work in reverse as well—once users start abandoning the platform, its usefulness declines very quickly. Look up what happened to MySpace if you don't believe me![10]

Exercises:

1. What are some examples of network effects around you that aren't related to business?
2. What are some examples of diseconomies of scale, where the larger you get the worse off you are?
3. Which of the following is an economy of scale, a network effect, or neither?
   a. A restaurant has a lot of customers, so it opens a second location.
   b. The Yankees can pay higher salaries than the Orioles.
   c. LinkedIn helps people find jobs, so many people post their resumes to the site, attracting corporate recruiters.
   d. A consultancy hires a new consultant for every three clients it signs.

ADVERSE SELECTION AND MORAL HAZARD

ADVERSE SELECTION AND MORAL HAZARD

Discipline: Economics

Summary: People with superior information can use it to their advantage. Thus, many business contracts are designed to prevent this from occurring, or at least be fairly compensated for the risk.

Why it is important: Information is power, and both are often unevenly distributed. You should try to make this work to your benefit or at least minimize its negative impact (i.e., don't be the sucker at the poker table!).

Example in discipline: The people who will have the most incentive to buy health insurance are the sickest—this is known as "adverse selection."

Once you buy car insurance, you will drive more recklessly than if you had no insurance at all—this is called "moral hazard."

Example outside discipline: If someone wants to sell you a used car, there is a chance that it is a lemon (a car that will break down a lot). The seller will likely know whether the car is better or worse than average for that model and vintage, while the buyer will not. Only sellers who believe their cars are worse than average will be willing to sell them for the average going price for that car—in other words, there is adverse selection. If the buyer negotiates a thirty-day, no-questions-asked, money-back guarantee to return the car in any condition, this may alleviate the adverse selection problem. However, there is then the risk that the buyer will treat the car badly before returning it a month later. This is a moral hazard.

Discussion: Asymmetric information is a large focus of economics, as most transactions take place with one party knowing more than the other. It begs the question: How do we reach an agreement about anything if we feel that we are constantly at risk of being played for a fool?

Insurance companies use all sorts of contract designs to eliminate adverse selection. Health insurance companies try to exclude pre-existing conditions,[11] life insurance companies employ their own teams of doctors to give physical exams, and property insurers use high deductibles (the amount that the policyholder must pay before the insurance starts paying out). There are also laws about what sorts of information must be disclosed when entering a financial contract, such as buying a piece of real estate. Despite this, adverse selection is present, and its cost must be incorporated into the price of the insurance.

It is important to consider the power of information asymmetry and how it can lead to suboptimal outcomes. Let's say that you plan on adopting a dog but first want to know if the dog is friendly. The shelter won't let you take the dog home for a trial period—it's "take it or leave it," they say. You cannot know ahead of time whether the dog is aggressive, since the shelter has the same policy for both mean and nice dogs. And so, you decide that adopting the dog is too risky, and the dog stays in the shelter. This is known as the "lemons problem," since the seller of the product usually knows more than the buyer, leading the buyer to assume the worst, and making the transaction difficult to complete.

Or let's say that you work at a consumer-lending startup. Your firm lends to consumers at rates a lot higher than they could get on a prime mortgage, but somewhat lower than they would pay on a credit card—say, 25 percent. Borrowers who are willing to pay this rate are statistically likely to default at an elevated level, but your firm has an algorithm that identifies those with only a 10 percent chance of not repaying the loan (versus those with a 50 percent chance). While only the borrowers really know their repayment intentions, lenders frequently will try to find clues in the financial record to help them make an educated guess.

Of course, information asymmetries can also work in your favor. If you know that you have a very large appetite, then all-you-can-eat sushi will be a great deal for you, and you should seek it out.[12] If you are going to drive across the country and back in a week, then you should rent a car with unlimited mileage, as it will be cheaper than driving your own vehicle.[13] And if you know that you have a habit of dropping your phone every few weeks, then you should buy the insurance!

Finally, you should be prepared to deal with asymmetric information, both to protect yourself from being taken advantage of and to credibly communicate with others that you are not trying to cheat them. If you deal with friends and family, then there is a bond of trust that usually compensates for this asymmetry. In business negotiations, doing business on a repeated basis allows for more trust, as it only takes one incident before you refuse to deal with someone again. Otherwise, a credible personal commitment, guarantee, or escrow arrangement will help close the gap. Finally, doing your research before making any big decisions—taking the used car to a trusted mechanic, getting reference checks on a potential renter, or speaking to several former employees before accepting a job offer—also goes a long way.

Exercises:

1. Health insurance companies, when they were enrolling older people for private Medicare plans, used to hold enrollment sessions on the second floor of a building with no elevator. Why might they do this?
2. A used car dealer is very honest and wants to convince potential customers that he is not selling lemons. How can he put his money where his mouth is?
3. A man whom you just met offers you a brand-new iPhone 15 for $200. It is sealed in the box so you cannot test it. Should you buy it?

BOTTLENECKS

BOTTLENECKS

Discipline: Business/operations

Summary: In any process, there is a limiting factor or scarce resource that determines the maximum rate of production. This is called the bottleneck.

Why it is important: Bottlenecks occur in manufacturing processes but also in many educational, athletic, and business situations. Look for the limiting factor and increase it in order to realize the greatest improvement.

Example in discipline: On a bottling line for soda, the filling machine can fill one hundred bottles per minute. The capping machine can cap 150 bottles per minute. Adding another capping machine wouldn't help to increase throughput, since the bottleneck is at the filling machine.

Example outside discipline: You buy a new laptop that has Intel's fastest processor but only 2 GB of RAM (working memory). The machine runs slowly since the RAM is not sufficient to take advantage of the processor's speed.

Discussion: A classic example of a bottleneck is that of a very slow-moving Boy Scout named Herbie[14] that slows down everyone behind him—the troop can only move as fast as he can. Helping him go faster (in this case, by distributing the contents of his backpack into others') is the only way to make the troop as a whole move more quickly. Bottlenecks are extremely common in manufacturing, computing, and other business situations, but there are also numerous examples of bottlenecks in one's personal life.

If the goal is to improve—your grades, a certain skill, your business—then the focus must be on the element that is the least developed and holding back the rest. For example:

- A piano sonata cannot be mastered until the hardest passage is played as smoothly as the easiest.
- If your memory is poor and you cannot remember the names of customers or coworkers, you need to develop a memory technique for this task.
- If you are working in a team, and one of the team members moves at a noticeably slower pace than the others, then the rest of the team must help (physically or intellectually) for the team to achieve its full potential (or the team member must be replaced).
- You want to grow your shrimp farming business, but there is a shortage of shrimp nets. You have customers and workers lined up for the expansion, but without the nets you cannot move forward.
- You resolved to make it home for family dinners this year, but you are chronically late due to an unpredictable commute. You need to free up time in the day or adopt a hybrid work arrangement to get home earlier.

Always looking for the weakest attributes and seeking to improve them will allow you to improve in many ways. To be clear, this is not a recommendation to dwell on negativity. But you should remember that humans have a natural reluctance to engage with their weaknesses, preferring the easier path of focusing on their areas of strength. However, this will not lead to improvement—the bottlenecks still exist, and Herbie isn't going to move any faster without some help!

Exercises:

1. Pencil manufacturing has three steps—making the pencil, attaching the eraser, and sharpening. The pencil maker generates 1,000 pencils/hour, the "attacher" can add 2,000 erasers/hour, and the sharpener can process 500 pencils/hour. What is the best way to increase the capacity of the manufacturing line?
2. You want to get 100 percent on an upcoming Spanish test. You have mastered verb conjugations, are decent at vocabulary, and are terrible at verbal comprehension. Where should you focus your studying efforts?
3. You are trying to make the varsity basketball team. You like practicing jump shots, since they usually go in, and other people are in the gym to see your prowess. However, you know that being able to hit a left-handed lay-up will be a necessary skill, one that you do not have. How should you spend your practice time?

5

Probability and Statistics

tatistics can be a dry topic, and as such it is frequently avoided like a proverbial plague. Unfortunately, the topic is complicated enough that if you don't have a decent grasp of it, you are at risk of being tricked. You may have even heard that statistics can be manipulated to "prove" anything, as described by the apocryphal quotation: "There are three kinds of lies: lies, damned lies, and statistics." Unfortunately, this is only one standard deviation away from the truth.

For the purposes of this book, we will skip over most of the math associated with statistics and instead focus on the principles behind them. These intuitions are very powerful and are used in almost every aspect of society—education, healthcare, engineering, government, finance, and dozens of other areas. The combination of this ubiquity and a high potential for abuse is what makes the understanding of statistics so important. No one likes to be misled, and I will help you appreciate what statistics can (and cannot) do.

Joined at the hip with statistics is its cousin, probability. Statistics is the process of analyzing data and drawing reasonable conclusions from it. Probability works in the opposite direction—predicting outcomes based on known rules. This comes in handy when playing games—board games, casino games, and card games—but also in real life, where good decisions cannot be made without understanding the range of possible outcomes and their likelihoods.

So, let's learn some statistics and probability. Heck, you may even enjoy it!

CORRELATION VERSUS CAUSATION

CORRELATION VS. CAUSATION

Discipline: Statistics

Summary: Given two sets of data that are positively correlated (tend to move in the same direction) with each other, and nothing else, it may be impossible to determine if the relationship is causal in one direction (A causes B), causal in the other direction (B causes A), or independent (A doesn't cause B, and B doesn't cause A).

Why it is important: Accepting correlation without understanding causality is a very dangerous intellectual mistake. The data may make you overconfident in the conclusion, even when they do not reveal causality. It is crucial to identify causality and have a reasonable explanation for why the correlation exists before making any decisions.

Example in discipline: A study shows that people who eat fish commit fewer violent crimes. The study implies that eating fish makes people more peaceful. However, an alternate explanation is that fish is relatively expensive and that, on average, the wealthier you are the less likely you are to commit a violent act.

Example outside discipline: On days with high sales of ice cream, many pairs of sunglasses are also sold. Do people wearing sunglasses like to eat ice cream, or do people eating ice cream like to wear sunglasses? Or is there another explanation (perhaps that it is a sunny day) that might explain both?

Discussion: In statistics, when two sets of variables or data move in the same direction, they are said to be "positively correlated." For instance, if you charted a child's daily consumption of nondiet soda versus the number of cavities they get, you would notice that there is a positive correlation—the more soda, the more cavities. In this case, the reason for the relationship is clear—soda contains sugar, and sugar causes cavities. This is called "causality"—one variable *causes* the other. However, there are many cases where causality is much less clear (figure 5.1). For instance, people who have dogs tend to have fewer allergies than people who don't. Is this because their immune systems' responses to allergens lessen with

FIGURE 5.1 Correlation does not equal causation. https://xkcd.com/552/.

greater exposure, or is it because people with bad allergies don't get dogs in the first place?

Unfortunately, it is not always possible to fully explain correlations. Variable A could cause Variable B, B can cause A, both could be caused by Variable C, or even some combination of these. Because of this, it is easy for an unscrupulous or lazy person to draw the conclusion that fits their agenda or needs. Furthermore, it is important to remember that statistics can show relationships that appear to be real but are in fact due to random chance (called "spurious relationships"). Given enough data, it is almost always possible to "data mine" to find a strong statistical relationship that is, in fact, nonsensical. In fact, someone has written an entire book on the topic with correlations such as this (figure 5.2).[1]

You should always keep in mind that drawing conclusions from statistics without an understanding of why the causal relationship exists can be extremely dangerous (especially in medicine, drug development, and public health). Recent developments in artificial intelligence and machine learning, for instance, have led to dangerous conclusions derived from spurious causality.[2]

Exercises:

1. In the Middle Ages, lice were believed to be beneficial to health, since there were rarely any lice found on sick people. The assumption was that the people would get ill if lice left their bodies. Knowing that lice are very

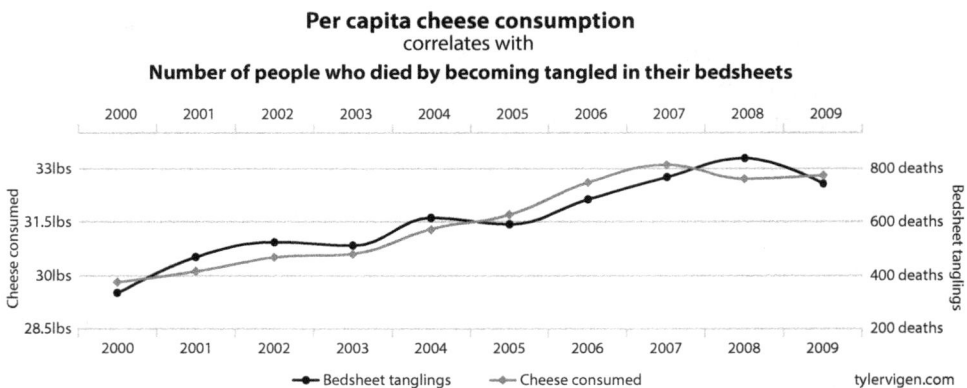

Per capita cheese consumption
correlates with
Number of people who died by becoming tangled in their bedsheets

FIGURE 5.2 Spurious correlation. https://www.tylervigen.com/spurious-correlations.

sensitive to the temperature of their host, what other explanation could you propose for this finding?

2. Children who sleep with a light on when young are found to have much higher rates of nearsightedness as adults. Does a lighter sleeping environment cause myopia?

3. Higher ice cream sales are found to be associated with more drowning deaths. Should you convince your town to outlaw ice cream?

STATISTICAL SIGNIFICANCE

STATISTICAL SIGNIFICANCE

Discipline: Statistics

Summary: Analyzing a sample from a large dataset may or may not allow you to draw accurate conclusions about all the data. Unless you analyze every piece of data, which is typically impractical, you must accept that your sample may not be representative of the whole, and any conclusions drawn from the sample could be incorrect.

Why it is important: Statistics permeate many aspects of life—personal (medical and dietary questions), professional (healthcare, finance, manufacturing, basic science, and professional sports) and regulatory/government (epidemiology, as a recent example) to name a few. Statistics should endeavor to reveal true relationships but can also be manipulated to lead to false conclusions. Knowing when statistics are applied correctly—and are therefore significant and meaningful—is an important skill to have.

Example in discipline: There are 100,000 salmon in a fish farm. A worker uses a net to catch two hundred of the salmon, which are then weighed. The farm then calculates the average (mean) weight of these two hundred fish, as well as how likely it is that these fish are representative of all the salmon at the farm (a range called the "confidence interval").

Example outside discipline: A clinical trial includes only twenty patients, ten of which receive the drug and ten of which receive a placebo. While seven of the patients who receive the drug show improvement in their symptoms, compared to five in the placebo group, this difference is not large enough to be statistically significant and could have been due to chance variation. As a result, the drug is not approved by the FDA.

Discussion: When thinking about a large dataset, the most intuitive descriptive statistic is the mean (average) of all values. The range, or variance of the data—how widely spread out the observations are around that average—is a little less obvious, but also fairly simple to grasp. Both summary statistics can be quite helpful—a river that has an average depth of 5 feet, with a range of 4 to 6 feet, is much safer to cross than one with the same average depth but a range of 2 to 12 feet. The concept that incorporates both metrics is known as statistical significance.

There are many situations in life where it is only feasible to gather a small sample of data, for example, when giving experimental drugs to human subjects. It is therefore important to specify whether that sample can be depended upon to represent reality—otherwise the whole exercise is kind of pointless. Statistics gives us the ability to take a sample of data, calculate the mean and variance of that sample, and then conclude how likely it is that the sample is, in fact, a good description of the whole. The bigger the sample, the more indicative it is likely to be, but real-world samples are expensive to collect, so smaller is better from that perspective.

With the mean and variance in hand, we can then calculate something called a "confidence interval," which is the range in which we are highly assured that the true value lies. In other words, it is very difficult to be sure that the average weight of an American male is precisely 180.25 pounds. Instead, we can be 99 percent confident that the average weight is between 176 and 184 pounds, assuming our sampling method is representative of the general population. Graphically, we use the simplifying idea of a bell curve and look for the area "under the curve" (figure 5.3).

An example may be helpful here. When trying to estimate the weight of all the dogs in the United States (roughly 100 million of them), we could randomly call veterinarians and animal shelters and ask them for the weights of all their dogs. Say that we get 100,000 data points by using this approach. The mean (average) is 28 pounds, and the standard deviation (one measure of variance) is 4 pounds. Knowing that ~95 percent of observations are within two standard deviations,[3] we can say that 95 percent of dogs weigh between 20 and 36 pounds [28 − (2 × 4) to 28 + (2 × 4)]. Since we have many data points (100,000), we have a high degree of confidence (over 99 percent) that this is very close to the range of the entire sample. If, however, we had only called one veterinarian and had gotten 100 dogs'

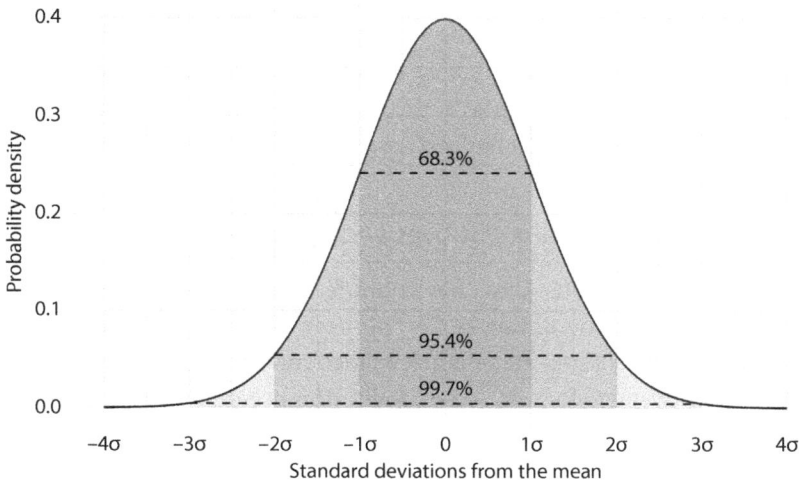

FIGURE 5.3 A normal distribution, or bell curve. Courtesy of D. Wells via Wikimedia Commons, CC BY-SA 4.0. https://commons.wikimedia.org/wiki/File:Standard_Normal _Distribution.png.

weights, we would have a much lower degree of confidence. The vet may serve an urban population that prefers smaller animals, for example, so the data would be biased in that direction.

It is equally important to remember that no matter how great the statistical confidence may be, samples are still not the whole. Unless we observe every datapoint, we cannot be totally sure that we haven't analyzed a biased subset. Say that a large jug contains 1,000 balls, of which ten are black. If we pick out ten balls from the jug and see five black ones, we might conclude (incorrectly) that half the balls are black—this is highly unlikely, to be clear, but it is possible. We must always be open to the possibility that the sample is misleading (in real life, this usually happens because the sampling method is biased, intentionally or unintentionally).

More generally, it is helpful to always keep in mind that *virtually every fact, decision or conclusion should have both a value and a confidence interval. Uncertainty is part of life,* and it is better to have this explicitly recognized and accounted for than assume that it does not exist. Will the sun rise tomorrow? Very likely, yes it will. But statistically, even that isn't a sure thing!

Karl Popper, a philosopher of science who was a great influence on George Soros, proposed the Falsification Principle. Any scientific theory must be testable, and if it is falsified, then it is shown to be untrue. However, the absence of falsification does not signal that the theory is true, since we just may not have found the falsifying evidence yet. Similarly, it is important to subject our strongly held beliefs to falsification on a regular basis and temper our conviction with the understanding that new information could and should lead to changed assumptions.

Corollary #1: False Positives and False Negatives

Given that any statistical analysis has room for error, there are two common errors that must be anticipated. The first is when the data doesn't comport with the predicted value but is in fact correct ("a false negative"), and the second is when data does agree with the predicted value but is in fact incorrect (a "false positive").

False positives and negatives are also especially important to understand in the context of medical testing (figure 5.4). During the COVID pandemic, some rapid antigen tests had false positive rates (where the test

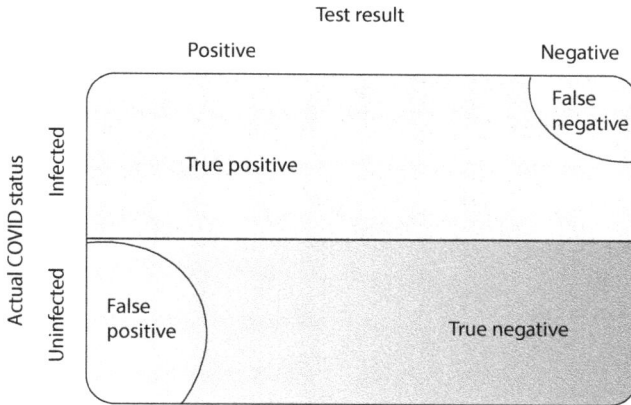

FIGURE 5.4 False positives and negatives in COVID-19 testing.

reads positive, but the person does not have COVID) of over 70 percent and false negative rates nearly as high, calling into question how useful these tests really were. Even very accurate tests can lead to poor conclusions if the incidence (percent of population with COVID) is low.

For example, say that the COVID incidence is 1 percent, so 1 of 100 people has COVID. If a test has a false positive rate of 10 percent, and 100 people without COVID are tested, their results will include 10 false positives and 1 true positive. So, the fact that someone tested positive still means that they are only 9 percent (1/11) likely to actually have COVID, rendering the test basically useless.[4]

Corollary #2: The Map is Not the Territory

This is a good place to remind you that models are simplifications of the real world, even though they are usually accurate enough for most purposes. A map that shows only roads is perfectly adequate for navigating to a friend's house, for example, even though the map leaves out many features of the terrain, such as potholes or hills. Still, it is important to remember that maps and all models are inherently (and intentionally) inaccurate and can lead you to the wrong conclusion. The Mercator projection on most globes was chosen to facilitate navigation by ships, so in that sense

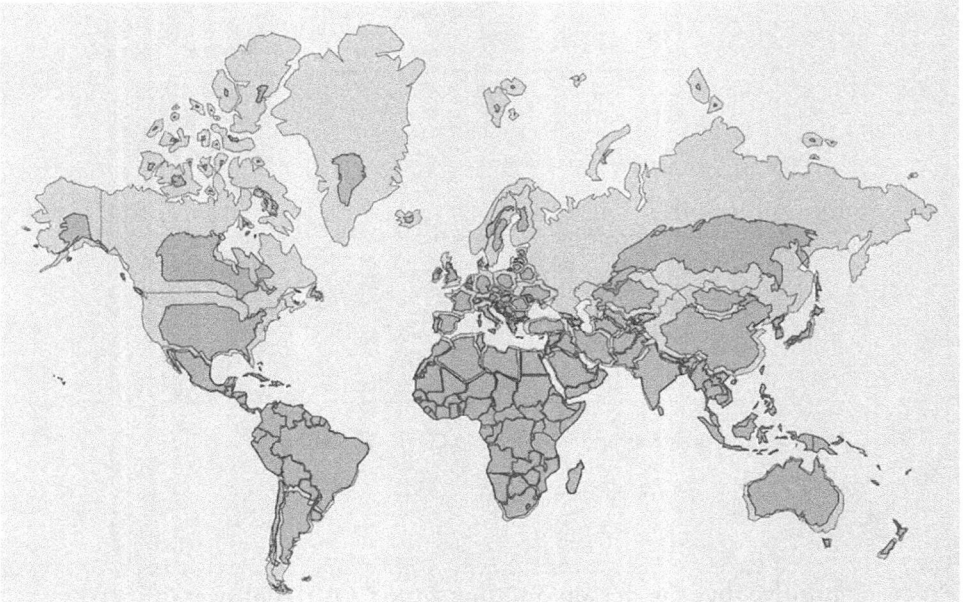

FIGURE 5.5 Mercator projection, unadjusted (light) and adjusted for actual sizes (dark). https://engaging-data.com/country-sizes-mercator/.

it was an optimal model. However, it also significantly distorts the relative size of countries, leading many people to believe that Greenland is as large as Africa, despite Greenland having only one-fourteenth the actual land area (figure 5.5).

Exercises:

1. A person draws five M&Ms from a jar, and they are all red. He states his belief that all the M&Ms in the jar are red. What is a reasonable response?
2. A scientific study shows that a new drug called Zoextra makes you live longer. When you read the study, though, you realize that the drug was only given to five patients. How should you react to this information?
3. You meet three Norwegians, and all are quite friendly and personable. Later, you meet three Swedes, who are generally irritable and argumentative. On this basis, what, if anything, should you conclude?

MEAN REVERSION

REVERSION TO THE MEAN

Discipline: Statistics

Summary: While some processes move in one direction, many return to an average value over time. Thus, extrapolating trends may lead to incorrect conclusions.

Why it is important: Humans are pattern followers and prone to believing that trends will continue. Statistically though, trends tend to reverse, and it is better to do nothing than "jump in" late. Psychological pressures make it difficult to resist this temptation.

Example in discipline: Investments that have higher-than-average returns for a ten-year period tend to have lower-than-average returns over the next ten years.

Example outside discipline: A new "growth" medicine is invented and given to children who are small for their age group when they are seven years old. Over the next few years, they grow twice as quickly as kids who were taller than average. The newspapers label this "growth" medicine a miracle drug. In fact, the medicine is a placebo, as smaller children tend to grow faster than average to catch up, while bigger kids grow more slowly, each reverting to the mean.

Discussion: As discussed in chapter 4 in the section on *economies of scale*, sometimes trends will be self-reinforcing, becoming more important as time passes. In the last fifty years, the rich have gotten richer and the powerful have gained more power (and applied that wealth and power within the political system to further benefit themselves). But much more commonly, the pendulum swings in the other direction and the trend reverses, which is called "reversion to the mean."

There are various reasons for why a trend will mean revert. Here are some examples of how it happens in practice:

Supply and demand: It costs $1 to grow an avocado, which typically sells for $2. If more people eat avocado toast (higher demand), the price of avocados may go up to $4, as there will be a shortage of avocados (especially in New York, Austin, and San Francisco). In response to this, avocado growers use more fertilizer and plant more avocado trees, such that the supply of avocados increases, which brings prices back down to $1.50 (oversupply). The lower price then encourages people to eat even more avocados, increasing demand, and bringing the market price back to $2.

Fashion trends: Kids loved fidget spinners, Rainbow Looms, and Squishmallows. They bought dozens of them, in all shapes and colors, until they grew bored of them. Kids then stopped buying these faddish toys and instead bought others.

Investment math: Buying stocks usually provides an investment return of around 8 percent, which is driven by the underlying profits of the companies themselves. So, on average, the fundamental value of a company's stock will increase at around 8 percent per year, but in any given year the stock price can diverge significantly from this "fair value." After many years of 15 percent stock returns, for example, they may be so highly priced (versus their fundamental value) that the future expected return is now only 2 percent a year. Investors recognize this, so they sell stocks, and stock prices go down. Eventually, if they decline enough, the prospective returns are again 8 percent (or higher).

Psychology and human nature: John and Jane usually get similar grades on tests. When John starts doing worse, he studies more. Meanwhile, Jane is getting straight A's, so she decides she can study less. Their test scores converge back at the same level. In financial markets, bubbles are formed as investors are lulled into complacency by rising prices and take greater risks as a result. Eventually, this goes too far, investments are made where the risk is far greater than the prospective rewards, and people lose a lot of money. The process may unwind in a spectacular fashion.

Biological processes: A child is predicted to be 5'7" based on the height of her parents. By age 7, she has grown much faster than expected and, based on her height at that age, is predicted to grow to be 6 feet tall. However, she stops growing much earlier than expected and ends up being 5'7" after all. Many biological processes are self-correcting in a similar manner.

Societal factors: The social and economic theory of Marxism predicts that while capitalism leads to the concentration of wealth in the hands of the few, eventually the poorer masses revolt and take back the wealth from the elite that controls it.[5] In other words, capitalism sows the seeds of its own destruction when it concentrates wealth in the hands of too few, as the "many" will ultimately reject this outcome and reconstitute society (through voting or through violence) in a fairer manner. Wealth is redistributed and society is restructured.

These were a lot of examples, across many disciplines, but the important takeaway here is that life has a way of self-correcting. This is not to say that life is fair—it is not! Nor am I saying that every process will mean revert. However, frequently there are mechanisms in place that tend to return the system to some stable value.

Exercises:

1. Your financial advisor calls you up and recommends that you buy a certain investment fund that has done particularly well for the last eight years. How do you respond?
2. Within reason, your metabolism adapts to keep your body weight roughly constant. If you are consuming a lot of calories, your body will burn them more quickly, and if you are consuming very few calories, your body will slow down its internal processes. So, if you gain a few pounds over the holidays, what's your best strategy to lose them?
3. You are playing blackjack and have seen a lot of low cards dealt. How should you change your playing strategy now?

PROBABILITY

Discipline: Statistics

Summary: There are no certainties in the world, just probabilistic outcomes. From the atomic scale to the development of the universe, probabilities shape our lives.

Why it is important: Most of life contains an element of probability or what many might call luck. Appreciating this fact and learning to be comfortable with a range of possible outcomes (all of which are within the realm of probability) will allow you to anticipate and adapt to life's various challenges.

This section will be laid out a bit differently from the others. Instead of giving a few examples of probability and then a few paragraphs of discussion, I will lay out the fundamental characteristics of probability and a series of examples that illustrate each of them. Becoming comfortable with probability is an important skill, and if this section is not clear, you should take additional steps to bolster your understanding. As such, I recommend some books and online resources in the endnotes that I believe are useful.

Here are the fundamental concepts of probability:

1. *General definition of probability*: The probability of a specific event occurring is the number of ways it could possibly happen divided by the number of total potential outcomes. Rolling two standard six-sided dice can produce 36 different combinations (shown in figure 5.6). Since there are six different ways for the dice to add to 7 (1 & 6, 2 & 5, 3 & 4, 4 & 3, 5 & 2, and 6 & 1), the probability of rolling a 7 with 2 dice =
   6 ways to roll a 7 divided by
   36 possible combinations from rolling 2 dice
   = 6/36 or 1/6 ≈ 16.7%.
   Probabilities are always between 0 and 1, which covers the range of impossible (0 percent) to certain (100 percent).
2. *Basic probability*: If you flip a fair coin, it will come up heads ½ of the time and tails ½ of the time (figure 5.7). If you choose a Bingo ball from a cage

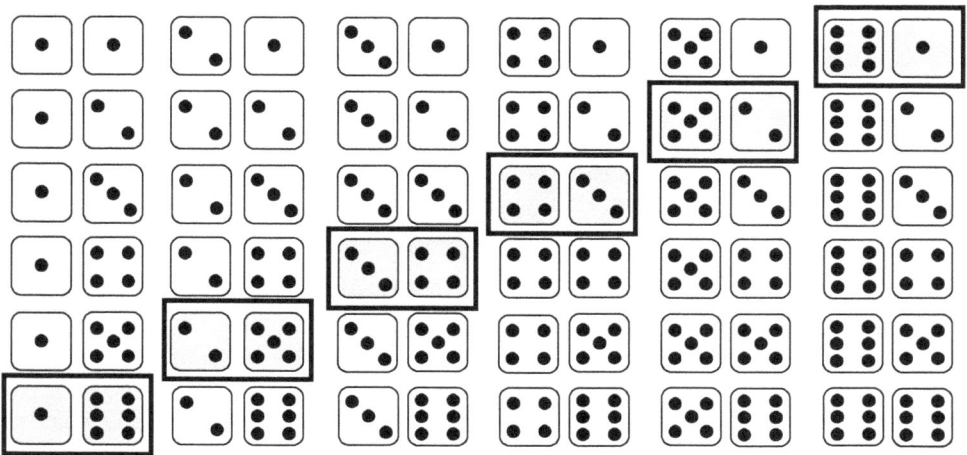

FIGURE 5.6 Possible combinations of two dice.

FIGURE 5.7 The basic probability of flipping a coin.

that contains every ball, each of the 75 numbers has a 1/75 probability of being drawn.

3. *Multiplicative property of probability*: The chance of multiple independent events all happening together requires multiplying the probabilities of each individual event happening alone. If the genetic chance of having a redheaded child is 1/9 and the chance of having a girl is 1/2, then the chance of having a redheaded girl is 1/9 × 1/2, or 1/18. Flipping a coin twice and getting two heads happens 1/4 of the time (½ × ½); flipping it three times and getting all heads happens 1/8 of the time (½ × ½ × ½). Figure 5.8 shows the eight equally likely ways that you can flip a coin three times—you can see that the three-heads result is one of these eight outcomes.

4. *Law of large numbers and distributions*: Even though a coin flip should produce a head 50 percent of the time, any single coin flip will either be a head or a tail—in other words, either 100 percent heads, or 0 percent heads. Any two flips could be one of four outcomes: HH, TT, TH, or HT, which corresponds to 100 percent heads, 100 percent tails, or 50 percent heads/tails. Thus, for a small number of trials or repetitions, the experienced probabilities can differ significantly from the predicted ones. However, after thousands of coin flips, it is highly likely that roughly half of the flips are tails and half are heads (figure 5.9). It is still very unlikely that you will get *exactly* 50 percent heads, but you will get close, and the more times you flip, the closer you will get.

5. *Inverse probability*: The chance of something *not* happening is 1 minus the chance of it happening. If I have a 1 percent chance of winning a raffle, then I have a 99 percent chance of *not* winning the raffle.

FIGURE 5.8 Multiplicative property of probability.

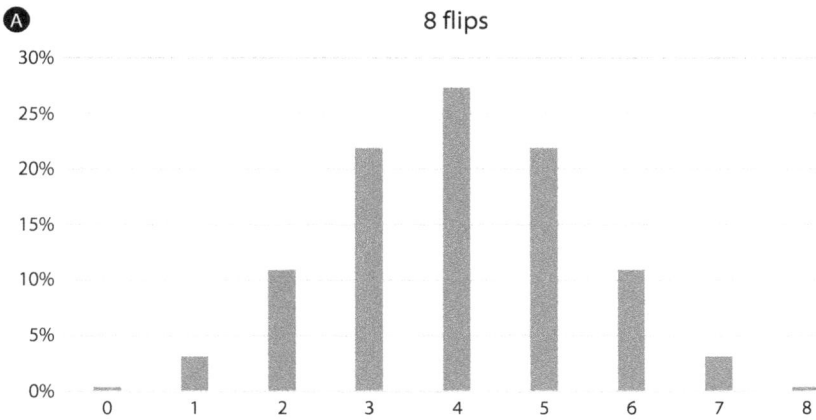

FIGURE 5.9A–D The law of large numbers.

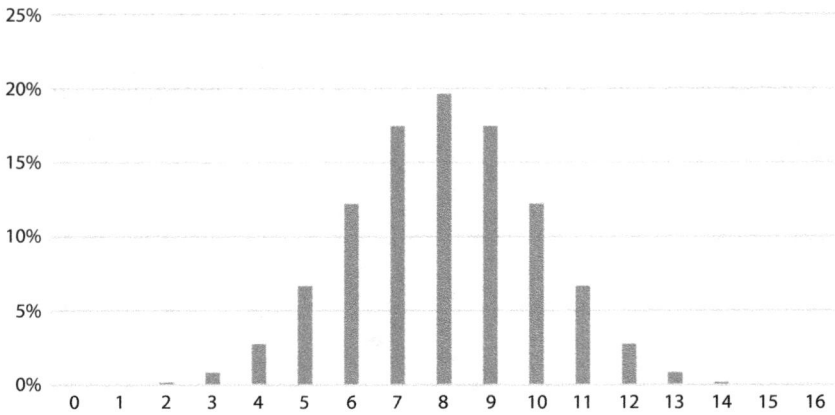

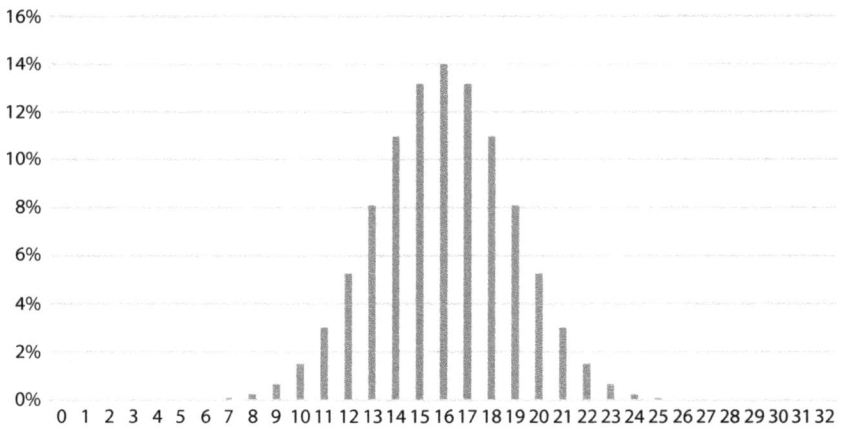

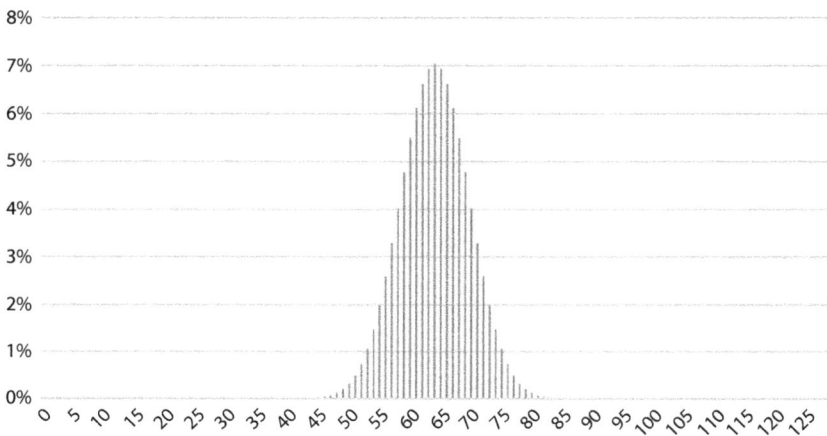

FIGURE 5.9A–D (*continued*)

6. *Conditional probability*: If you draw a single black ball out of a closed jar, you cannot know what mix of white and black balls is in the jar. If you draw 50 black balls in a row, though, you can safely assume that most or all the balls in the jar are black and that the next ball you draw is very likely to also be black (figure 5.10).

7. *Base rates*: Both absolute levels and percentage changes matter. A 10× change matters very much for an event that has a 5 percent likelihood and very little for an event with a .001 percent chance of occurring. In the first case, the 5 percent event became a 50 percent likelihood, while the .001 percent chance is still only .01 percent likely.

FIGURE 5.10A–B Balls in jars. DALL-E.

FIGURE 5.10A–B (*continued*)

If you hear that Steve is shy and had to guess whether he is a salesman or a librarian, you might be tempted to say that he is a librarian. However, there are only 160,000 librarians in the U.S. and 100 times as many sales-people, so Steve is much more likely to be a shy salesman than a librarian (figure 5.11)! The main importance of this concept is to trust the data—if something is very unlikely to happen, then despite any narratives you might hear, it still probably did not happen!

Discussion: Why is probability important? Because while statistics describe what has already happened and whether we should consider it important or disregard it, probability gives us a system for predicting future outcomes. This is important for games, investing, medicine, and many professional and leisure activities. For example:

1. A certain medical procedure (a test for cancer) has a complication rate of 1/20 (e.g., the biopsy itself may cause an infection) and a false positive rate

FIGURE 5.11 Base rate fallacy. https://thedecisionlab.com/biases/base-rate-fallacy.

of 1/10 (the test will tell you that you have cancer 10 percent of the time, even when you don't). Under what circumstances might it not be a good idea to have the procedure done?

When the risk of getting cancer is so low that the risk of complications is much higher than the chance of getting the disease.

2. You are playing five card draw poker and have three queens. You think you need four queens to win. What are the chances of drawing another queen?

Only 1 of the 49 remaining cards is a queen, but you have two chances to draw it, so you have roughly a 2/49 chance (or ~4 percent).

3. You are deciding what insurance to buy for your dog. You know that, statistically, your dog will go to the vet once a year and it will cost $200 for that visit. There is a 1 percent chance that your dog will need to go to a pet hospital, which would cost $10,000. Do you buy a policy that costs $500 a year but covers all expenses, or one that costs $100 but has a $200 deductible (you must pay $200 before your insurance starts paying anything) and only pays 50 percent of expenses (called the coinsurance)?

The first insurance costs you $500/year, and this amount is fixed. The second will vary but is expected to cost $100 premium + $200 (the $200 visit isn't covered due to the deductible) + $50 (1% × $10,000 × 50%) = $350 per *year, so the second one is a better deal. Not buying insurance is expected to cost you $200 + $100 (1% × $10,000) = $300, so it is an even better deal, assuming the pet hospital bill isn't more than $10,000.*

4. A large asteroid is hurtling toward earth. What are the chances it will make a direct impact?

   Well, the math is very complicated, but you could model all possible paths that the asteroid could take and then count which ones make it collide with earth. The answer seems to be around one in a million, based on an online search.

5. Ford is deciding whether to recall a model of car for a known steering defect. They predict that the failure rate will be .01 percent (so, for 100,000 cars, 10 will fail), and that the cost of each failure will be $500,000 (people aren't likely to die, but there will be accidents, and Ford will have to settle with the cars' owners). The cost of a full recall and replacement of the steering system is $1,500 per car. What should Ford do?

   Putting morality aside, they realize for economic purposes that the cost of a recall is $150 million, while the cost of dealing with lawsuits is only $5 million, so they do not issue a recall.

6. You are considering entering a school raffle. The prize is a new car (worth $30,000), the tickets cost $20, and you estimate that they have sold 300 tickets. The drawing is coming up in a few minutes. Should you buy a ticket?

   Yes, you should buy a lot of tickets, assuming it's a car you want! If you spend $1,000 on tickets, for example, you will have a 1/7 (50 out of 350) chance of winning the car, which is worth $30,000. The expected value of these tickets is thus 1/7 × $30,000 or $2,100, while the cost was $1,000. That having been said, most raffles and lotteries have very negative expected values!

7. My daughter is applying to 12 colleges, and her chances of being accepted at each are roughly 10 percent. My wife is concerned that she won't be accepted anywhere—should she be worried?

   The chances of getting rejected from every school is the chance of not getting into each school (90 percent), multiplied together 12 times, so .9 × .9 × .9 × .9 × .9 × .9 × .9 × .9 × .9 × .9 × .9 × .9. This works out to 28 percent, so she has a 72 percent chance of getting into at least one school. This assumes that the 10 percent chance at each college is an independent probability, though.

8. The chances of getting audited by the IRS for not paying enough taxes are .5 percent or 1/200. You are deciding whether to take a legitimate $1,000

deduction, but one for which you have lost the receipt. If you get audited, you will have to pay back the $1,000 as well as $500 in penalties. Do you take the deduction?

Yes, the penalty is relatively low considering how unlikely the audit is.

9. You see a raccoon in the yard, and your friend is scared that the animal is rabid and asks you to stay indoors. You decide that this is unlikely and chase the animal away, after reading that there has only been one recorded death from raccoon-borne rabies, ever.[6]

This is totally a rational decision. However, the raccoon could still scratch and bite you, and rabies shots are painful!

10. You read that the average life expectancy is 81 for women, and you are 80 years old. You believe that you only have 1 year left to live. Is this correct?

No, you forgot about conditional probability. The 81-year average is for people of all ages, including those who have died earlier; the life expectancy for females that have already made it to 80 is 90 years old, or ten more years.

11. The FDA is considering approving an expensive ($1,000) vaccine that will reduce the chance of getting a rare disease by 50 percent. However, upon doing a little research, they realize only 1/100,000 people get the disease. Should they approve the drug?

No. If the whole country took the drug, the number of people with the disease would drop from 3,000 to 1,500, but this would cost $300 billion.

There is something both constraining and freeing about understanding the importance of probability. Our lives are neither predetermined (by a divine being or by anything else) nor fully in our control (as randomness plays a role in every aspect of them). At the same time, even entirely random processes are predictable within a range of outcomes. Once you start thinking in probabilistic terms, you will not feel as bad about decisions that turn out poorly, nor as good about certain accomplishments where luck played a role.

And luck always plays some role. In the early days after founding FedEx, Fred Smith was denied a business loan and couldn't pay his fuel bills. He stopped in Las Vegas, turned $5,000 to $27,000 at the blackjack table, and kept the company afloat until he could raise more money.[7] I bet Fred appreciates the role that luck played in his career!

Interlude

We have now discussed thirty-two important concepts and just knowing them will greatly increase your understanding of many different fields. But that was just the beginning! Now we will utilize these concepts as the foundations of five different frameworks, each of which should allow you to make a meaningful improvement in your intellectual interactions and success. Before we do this though, let's look at table I.1 for a preview of which concepts are most relevant for each of the frameworks we are going to discuss.

Table I.1 Application of concepts to frameworks

	Decisions	Learning	Understanding	Investing	Happiness
Cognitive biases					
Self-esteem	x	x	x	x	x
Stories (not statistics)	x	x	x	x	x
Snap judgments	x	x	x	x	x
Liberal arts					
Mind-body connection	x				x
Utilitarianism	x				x
Hierarchy of needs	x				x
The Golden Rule	x				

Table I.1 (*continued*)

	Decisions	Learning	Understanding	Investing	Happiness
Reciprocity	x		x		
Occam's razor	x	x			
Inversion	x	x	x	x	x
Perspective	x	x	x	x	x
Investing and science					
Expectations	x			x	x
Risk versus reward	x			x	
Compound interest	x	x		x	
Checklists	x	x	x	x	x
Redundancy	x			x	x
Feedback loops	x	x			
Activation energy		x			x
Decision versus outcome	x		x	x	x
Leverage	x	x			x
Business and economics					
Sunk cost	x	x			x
Expected value	x			x	
Incentives	x	x	x	x	x
Declining marginal utility	x	x	x	x	x
Negotiations	x				
Comparative advantage	x	x			x
Game theory and deductive reasoning	x	x	x		x
Network effects and economies of scale		x		x	
Adverse selection and moral hazard	x			x	
Bottlenecks	x	x			x
Probability and statistics					
Causation versus correlation	x		x	x	
Statistical significance	x		x	x	
Mean reversion	x		x	x	
Probability	x		x	x	

As you can see, the decisions framework draws on nearly every concept discussed. This makes sense as decision-making is an incredibly wide-ranging activity and all our mental faculties (and biases) come into play. The rest are more balanced, with each framework relying on roughly half of the concepts. For the sake of brevity, I will not refer to every concept in the discussion of frameworks, but it is helpful to keep them in mind, nonetheless. Additionally, some concepts aren't all that relevant to these frameworks but are important to have learned for other reasons.

After we have taken a brief *pause to think*, let's begin our discussion of important frameworks!

PART II

IMPORTANT FRAMEWORKS

6

Decisions

DECIDING

I USE THIS LUCKY COIN FOR ALL MY DECISIONS.

EVEN THE IMPORTANT ONES?

ESPECIALLY THE IMPORTANT ONES! I ALWAYS REGRET IT WHEN I DON'T.

IT'S IMPORTANT NOT TO REGRET YOUR DECISIONS BUT ISN'T THERE A BETTER PROCESS?

MY GREAT GRANDFATHER USED THIS COIN WHEN HE WAS AUDITIONING THE BEATLES.

WELL, THAT WAS A GOOD DECISION! OR, AT LEAST, A GOOD OUTCOME...

ACTUALLY, THE COIN CAME UP TAILS AND HE DECIDED NOT TO SIGN THEM. BUT HE STILL LOVED THIS COIN.

YEAH, THE BEATLES WERE OVERRATED ANYWAY.

As I just mentioned, the area that incorporates most of the concepts is decision-making, so let's start there. Each day, we make dozens of decisions. Some of these are minor, such as what to eat for breakfast, while others are major, such as whether to ask someone to marry us. Mostly, we use a combination of rational thinking, gut feelings, and external inputs—some explicitly solicited from trusted friends and family and others subconsciously internalized as expectations or social norms. While people use well-developed systems to solve many problems in their lives—doing long division, troubleshooting computer problems, and diagnosing illnesses—they tend not to when making decisions, which seems like a tremendous oversight.

This chapter discusses a framework which works well for me, though it may not work perfectly for you if followed exactly as written. More important than the exact steps laid out below is an appreciation of these general principles, so that you can vary the application of those ideas and adjust when appropriate. There are many books written solely about decision-making, so you can get as deep into this topic as you want! But this approach is flexible enough that it should work well for a range of decisions.

To start, here are the core principles for decision-making:

1. Determine whether the decision itself justifies the time spent using a structured framework.
2. Gather as much data as is practically possible around the decision.
3. Strive to have several options from which to choose, but not more than four lest the "paradox of choice" set in.
4. Actively ignore mental biases where your subconscious is "tricking" you into focusing on the wrong aspects of a decision.
5. Be explicit about what expectations are at work, both yours and those of important third parties.
6. Make the decision that, based on the information you have at the time, you are least likely to regret.
7. Embrace your emotional self and make the final decision based on your "gut" feeling after reviewing all the information.

In summary, we have:

Satisficing versus deep dive
Information gathering
Narrow down the choices
Checklist of concepts and biases
Explicit expectations
Regret minimization
Embrace emotion

And it is my **SINCERE** hope that you remember this acronym!

The key to this acronym is to follow it in order. If you decide that the decision is not that meaningful, then it probably isn't necessary to spend any time on the rest of the steps. If you don't have enough information, you can't intelligently narrow down your choices, and so on.

If you take a step back, you will see that this approach breaks the process down into three phases:

Phase 1. Determine the importance of the decision: This is where you ask your-self how much time and effort to spend on making the decision. If the decision is unimportant or easily reversible, then it's not worth spending much time on it; make a "satisficing" decision and move on. Overthinking decisions (aka "analysis paralysis") should be avoided!

Phase 2. Research the decision: This is where you gather information, narrow it down to a few choices, and check that your cognitive biases aren't impair-ing your decision-making process.

Phase 3. Gut check: You have a preliminary decision now, but you need to make sure you feel good about it. Consider this decision against your expecta-tions, anticipate whether your future self will regret your choice, and see if your emotional brain has anything to add.

Let's now go through each of the steps.

SATISFICING VERSUS DEEP DIVE

Not all decisions are equally important, and we make thousands of deci-sions every day that shouldn't be agonized over (PB&J or tuna for lunch? Red or green socks?). There are two aspects of a decision that make it worthy of more consideration: Will it have a large impact on your life (and those around you), and is it difficult to reverse after it is made? If the answers to both questions are "yes," then you should invest the time to make a proper decision. If either is "no," then make a "satisficing" or "good enough" decision and move on with your life! Even for these smaller decisions, though, I still believe that you should use a regret minimization framework but apply it with a little less rigor (in other words, lightly consider steps 2 through 5 but ultimately jump to step 6).

INFORMATION GATHERING

This part is straightforward but probably takes the most time. Simply put, you should gather the most relevant data possible before forming an opinion. Employing the Pareto principle as a rough guide, you should only stop when you have gathered 80 or 90 percent of this information (hopefully, with only 20 or 30 percent of the work!). If you can read some professional reviews of products you are buying, you should do so. If there is someone who might be able to offer you some valuable insight, you should reach out to that person and try to gather multiple perspectives whenever possible. If there are specific issues that you don't quite understand, you should figure them out before deciding. And, of course, be aware of your cognitive biases, which will affect how and why you gather certain information. Availability, confirmation, overconfidence, and framing will all lead you to overemphasize certain information and ignore salient facts.

Of course, not all data are good, and some should be ignored. There is an old computer programming saying, "garbage in, garbage out"—bad inputs into a good decision process will lead to poor decisions. Malcolm Gladwell's book *Talking to Strangers* gives numerous examples of how personal interactions can mislead us.[1] In it, he reminds us that career diplomats and CIA counterintelligence officials are frequently tricked, so we should assume that we can be also. Most people believe that they are good judges of character but frequently make worse decisions based on personal impressions than they do without any personal contact at all.

There is extensive evidence emerging that in-person job interviews are more an indication of likeability and extroversion than of job qualifications.[2] Additionally, these interviews bring significant bias into the hiring process, leading to the exclusion of certain candidates. Orchestras were under 6 percent female in 1970 before they moved to blind auditions; now they are 35–50 percent.[3] Moreover, interviewees frequently lie, and interviewers treat good-looking people more favorably.[4] It may seem odd to hire someone without meeting them first, but the data suggest that this is exactly what should be done. All of this means that you should be aware of your own biases and fallibilities when gathering data and more generally.[5]

If you applied to college, you may have spent some time visiting campuses. What information did you glean from these experiences? Was your opinion swayed by the weather, friendliness of the interviewer, or attractiveness of the tour guide? Of course it was—you are only human! Your single experience was likely to be misleading in at least a few ways, while the accumulated data of thousands of student surveys, course catalogues, and employment statistics paint a much more accurate picture of the institution.

As a corollary to this, remember to only solicit information from disinterested parties. A salesperson is unlikely to give you unbiased information. Ditto for Fox News or a conspiracy website! See chapter 8 for more about this.

NARROW DOWN THE CHOICES

It is nice to have options in life, but more is not always better in this regard. Research has shown that having a few choices makes you happier than having just one, since this will more closely match your preferences and achieve a near-optimal outcome. Too many choices, though, and you will overthink the decision. You will spend so much time comparing the multitude of choices that you subconsciously imbue the decision with more importance than it merits. You are more likely to get bogged down by all that information and end up procrastinating. Finally, since your choice will likely be inferior to the other options in some specific aspect, you have more potential to regret your decision (the paradox of choice).

It turns out that the saying "everything in moderation" applies here as well. The rule here is to limit yourself to four options. There is no great basis for this rule, to be honest. Three seems like too few, and five seems a bit unwieldy. That said, if you really want to use three or five, be my guest. But no more than five!

Constraints are likely to enter the picture as these options are considered. This is an engineering term, akin to *bottlenecks*, and refers to the natural limitations governing the decision. Cost is a common constraint, as are size and location. If you are cooking dinner, your constraints are the ingredients that you have in your house at the time, and if you are buying a car in Vermont, you should only consider four-wheel drive options. Clearly, you must subject your potential choices to any relevant constraints, or they are not feasible to begin with!

You won't be surprised to hear that it is possible to run a statistical analysis on each type of decision you might make and fine-tune your approach accordingly. This process is a bit too involved for this book, but the concept is worth considering. For example, when searching for an apartment, you should spend 37 percent of your allotted search time viewing different units but not signing a lease. After this, you should rent the first apartment you see that is better than all the previous ones,[6] which will provide a statistically optimal outcome. Still, while this is an interesting theoretical exercise, for most situations it is best to stick with four choices.

There are even those who try to eliminate choices to focus their mental attention on other matters. For example, Mark Zuckerberg famously wears only one outfit.

Note that the information gathering and choosing processes should be iterative to make them more efficient. Instead of doing exhaustive research on every possible choice, do some research on the most likely ones. Then, narrow it down and drill deeper into those four. If this research uncovers aspects of the choices that make them unsuitable, replace one or more of them and repeat the process.

CHECKLIST OF BIASES

Almost every one of the cognitive biases that we discussed in the first section of the book and most of the other concepts discussed in the earlier chapters come into play in decision-making. I will not rehash them here (since you just read all about them), but rather will remind you of the general categories of biases:

— We like to feel good about ourselves.
— We view the world using stories instead of statistics.
— We make instinctive judgments and then stick to them.

To avoid having these biases impair our decision-making ability, we must actively correct for them. For example:

— If we choose an easier career path because we want to feel good about ourselves and not risk failure, we will probably regret this decision in the long term, since we won't have pushed ourselves to our full potentials.

- If we take shortcuts to make a complicated decision easier, we may miss important information and make a poor decision as a result.
- Whenever we can make a probabilistic estimate of different outcomes, we should. We shouldn't put undue weight on these probabilities, but we shouldn't ignore them either.
- If we see ourselves making snap decisions, we should walk those biases back and start over, using our "slow" brain to make a more reasoned determination.

Just like our expectations, these biases are firmly lodged in our brains and must be actively addressed to be neutralized. The following checklist will help you to avoid falling prey to these biases as well as incorporate some of the other concepts discussed previously.

Am I making a choice that:

Makes me feel good about myself?
Is based on a narrative instead of data?
Is due to instinctive reaction instead of a reasoned process?
  If so, I should reevaluate the choice.

Can I improve the decision by focusing on:

Comparative advantages?
Mutual benefit?
Compounding?
Network effects?
Bottlenecks?
  If so, I should incorporate these and reframe the decision.

Am I remembering to consider:

Both the risks and rewards of the decision?
Redundancy and margin of safety?
All probable outcomes and expected values?
Mean reversion?
Second order effects?
Declining marginal utility?
The Golden Rule?
  If not, I should apply these concepts to my process.

And am I remembering to ignore:

Sunk costs?
Poor incentives?
Moral hazard?
Spurious correlation?
  If not, I will likely come to the wrong conclusion.

I want to highlight both the *Golden Rule* (how the decision impacts others) and the idea of *second order effects*, as these are particularly easy to overlook. Taking a new job that pays more might seem like a straightforward decision, but remember to think through the consequences. What will your existing colleagues and bosses think of the move? Will working at the new firm enhance your reputation or tarnish it? How will your children or life partner be affected by the change, and how will they alter their behaviors as a result? Will the higher pay bring with it more work hours, and what are the emotional and financial costs of that change? Decisions frequently impact others around you, and these concepts help to remind you of that fact.

EXPLICIT EXPECTATIONS

As we have seen earlier in the book, *expectations* play a crucial role in happiness. Whether or not you explicitly acknowledge them, you currently hold expectations around many aspects of your life, derived either internally or from the influence of others—family, friends, teachers, or coworkers. Exceeding these expectations will (temporarily) bring you happiness and falling short will (temporarily) bring you pain. Getting a $5,000 bonus would be a disappointment if you had expected $10,000 but a welcome surprise if you didn't expect a bonus at all.

However, expectations are neither static nor set in stone. If you decided to apply to medical school since this is what was "expected" of you by your parents, you may be miserable. But if you recognized this expectation and consciously decided to reject it and reset it, then you could have made a different decision. To do this, though, you must crystalize these expectations and make them *explicit*, since we frequently hold expectations for ourselves that we don't consciously understand or appreciate.

Usually, this discovery process will work in reverse (here is *inversion* again). In other words, as you are considering which outcomes you may regret in the future, you may find yourself disappointed by some choice without initially understanding why. After thinking about it further, though, you realize that the decision will lead you to an outcome that falls short of some expectation that you hold.

For example, say you are considering applying to graduate school to become a teacher. This career seems to "check all the boxes"—it is intellectually challenging, contributes to society, and allows you to work with children. But you still feel as though you will regret it and are not excited about the prospect. As you think about it more deeply and picture your future self as a teacher, you realize that you have always pictured yourself as accumulating more wealth, since your parents have frequently hinted that it would be nice to have a child who could support them financially as they got older. You then need to decide whether to embrace that expectation and think of another career (or a way to earn more money while still being a teacher) or reject it to pursue this one. Either decision is reasonable—the important point is to be explicit about which expectations are in place.

Setting expectations for yourself and having them set for you are normal and helpful parts of human existence. Making decisions without understanding which expectations are in place, though, is leaving out a big piece of information, like deciding on a new car without knowing the price. Put differently, this part of the process forces you to be honest with yourself about what you want and why you want it.

REGRET MINIMIZATION

At this point we need to ask ourselves how we define a "good" decision. You might think that a "good" decision is one that leads to a desirable outcome, but this is not correct. In fact, we cannot judge a decision solely by how it turns out, since as we saw earlier, it is very possible to make *a bad decision that leads to a good outcome*, and vice versa. This is the nature of a probabilistic world. We can be 95 percent sure of a given outcome and experience the 5 percent scenario regularly.

Annie Duke, a former professional poker player and current self-help consultant, wrote an excellent book on the topic of decision-making.[7] In it, she says:

> I've done this exercise with hundreds of people and it always turns out like this. When I ask for their best decision, they tell me their best outcome. When I ask for their worst decision, they tell me their worst outcome.

There are two issues at work here. The first is that it is easier to recall outcomes (which are concrete) than decision-making processes (which are abstract), and so a bad decision with a good outcome will be favorably remembered, to the detriment of future decision-making processes. A larger point though is that outcomes *cannot* be fully controlled. And so, the basis on which we should judge our choice must depend on the integrity of the decision-making process itself. The surest way that I have found to do this is through the concept of *regret minimization*.

Regret is a powerful human emotion, whether it is FOMO on a great party that you decided to skip or a stock that doubles in price after you didn't buy it. It is all around us, and it sucks, doesn't it? So, trying to reduce regret whenever possible seems like an intuitively good thing to do. But why will it lead us to make better decisions?

Here's why: any decision we make will lead to some outcome (that, again, we cannot fully control). This outcome may be good or bad, and even an outcome that we thought was good could turn out badly (and vice versa). You might think that veterinary school is the perfect fit for you and end up hating all those whiny, fluffy kittens. There is just no way to know a) with certainty and b) ahead of time which outcomes will transpire, and whether those outcomes will be truly desirable when they happen.

But what if we could be sure (within reason) that we are *doing our very best* to avoid outcomes that would be bad for us (again, the concept of *inversion*)? Think of a time when you have practiced hard, played your heart out, and still lost to a more skilled opponent—you could still be proud of your effort and accomplishment. In the same way, if you are confident that the decision you made *was the best that you could possibly have made* given what you knew at the time, then it will be hard for you to regret that decision. After all, you worked hard and did your best! And, over a lifetime of making hundreds of similar decisions, the odds will be in your favor that your well-honed process will lead to excellent outcomes.

Effectively, you are having a conversation with your future self that goes something like this:

FUTURE SELF: "Why did you decide to take this job?"
PRESENT SELF: "Given everything I knew at the time, I believed that I would be least likely to regret that choice."
FUTURE SELF: "But it turns out that this job is terrible."

PRESENT SELF: "I know, it's a shame. But there is no way I could have known that at the time. I made a thorough and reasoned decision and wouldn't change anything about the process. Sometimes life turns out differently than we expect. It is complicated and somewhat random, so we can't predict it all that well."

FUTURE SELF: "Present Self, you make a convincing argument. I guess I'm okay with the decision after all. But seriously, we need to find a new job!"

This is basically the conversation that Jeff Bezos, a famous proponent of the regret minimization framework, had with himself before deciding to start Amazon. It seems like it worked out pretty well for him . . .

By adopting this framework, we are implicitly acknowledging that life's outcomes are probabilistic. We are not in full control of our fates and chance will play a role, though of course with hard work we can maximize the former and minimize the latter. Expected values combine this probability with the desirability of each outcome, and the law of large numbers ensures that over time we will be compensated for accepting this randomness. But only by appreciating the role that luck plays will we be able to make regret-minimized decisions.

EMBRACE YOUR GUT

This last step may (and should) seem surprising, given that much of this book has centered around using conscious mental frameworks to counteract irrational (and at times, emotional) biases. But remember that our brains evolved to assimilate a huge amount of information and then make decisions that would increase our odds of survival. That "gut" feeling you have is actually a simple way for your brain to communicate a summary of all the information it has gathered. To ignore one's gut would be to ignore a very important piece of data.

Let me be clear though—this only works if you have already gathered a lot of information that can accurately "feed" your intuition's algorithm. I am *not* saying that you should use your gut intuition *instead* of all the other steps discussed above. But sometimes external data can be misleading, and thus there is always a possibility that the "rational" decision is based on flawed information. Your intuition should be viewed as the final (pardon the pun) "gut-check."

For instance, you might gather a lot of data that supports taking a job at a certain company. But when you meet the CEO, you feel that he is highly untrustworthy. You probably shouldn't work there, even if the data tell you otherwise. Your information could be wrong, the workplace may be toxic, and you might be stuck in a bad situation. There would certainly be a high potential for regret.

Or you may scour Consumer Reports and decide to buy a new Smart car. All the numbers seem great, and the car will likely be highly functional in an urban environment. But your intuition tells you that you will hate it, since you will always be nervous that a truck will flatten you like a pancake. Don't buy that car, as you will likely regret it!

This also holds when deciding whether to date someone. They may look "good on paper"—smart, good looking, and athletic—but if there is something about them that makes you nervous, then stay away. Your gut knows!

BUYING A CAR

Let's put **SINCERE** into practice.

Clearly, purchasing a car is a big decision, having significant financial ramifications, and it is difficult to reverse without large frictional costs. So, it is not a decision that can be "satisficed," and it must be analyzed with more care. We should move on to the information-gathering phase of the process.

There is a lot of information about cars out there, so this will be an iterative process. Start by selecting four models based on what you think you know about your needs: size of car, drivetrain (EV, ICE, or hybrid), cost to buy or finance it, performance, and annual operating costs.

For each of the models you selected, investigate the following attributes:

– Safety features.
– Reliability and expected maintenance costs.
– Features such as 4WD and mileage.

Websites such as edmunds.com, kbb.com, and consumerreports.org are good places to go for unbiased reviews. Read these reviews and look at the safety and reliability ratings for each car. Now decide if the four cars you selected still make sense or if one or more of them should be ruled out based on this information. If so, replace these models with alternatives and repeat the process.

Once you have chosen the car models, though, the decision gets complicated, as you now must compare new and used cars from different years, all being sold by different dealers. For instance, you might want to consider a Honda CRV, a Toyota RAV-4, and a Ford Escape, which are three different cars. But really you need to compare each of these cars, with different trim levels and optional features, from different model years, with different mileages. This could mean hundreds of different combinations, which makes it far too difficult of a decision!

So, let's narrow it down some more. Cost is the easiest variable on which to set a limit (constraint). Say your absolute maximum is $30,000. Before taxes and various fees, this means you need to select a car that has a list price of $26,000 or less. Set this as a maximum in an online automobile search engine, input the models you have chosen, and decide based on your research which model years are acceptable (some years are more reliable than others, and styling also can vary from year to year). Now make sure the car has the safety features that you require. If possible, only look for cars that have under 40,000 miles on them, as those will be less likely to have serious reliability issues imminently.

After all this, it's time to test drive at least one of each model. You might find that certain cars are more difficult to drive or you can't see well through the back window. Incorporate these data points and narrow the list down further if possible.

Now consult your *checklist*. The main risks in this situation are buying a car that is too expensive for your budget (no financial *margin of safety*), buying a car that is fun but not practical (falling for a *narrative*), and being on the wrong end of an information asymmetry (*adverse selection*). Make sure you are addressing these cognitive biases and using tools such as warranties or seller guarantees to avoid getting a lemon.

At this point, you should make your *expectations explicit* by discussing with your partner (or parents) what the budget is and whether there are certain types of cars that are off limits. Be honest with yourself about what sort of car you will feel comfortable driving—is a minivan out of the question, and do you need that two-ton lifted pickup truck?

As always, you need to make sure that you have *minimized regret*. Picture yourself in each of the cars a few years from now. Something has gone wrong—the car keeps breaking down, it isn't meeting your needs (not enough interior space, perhaps), or it's costing a lot more than you thought for gasoline. Could you have foreseen any of this? If not, then you have no reason to regret the purchase. Congratulations, this seems like a good choice!

Now you are ready to *embrace emotion.* Which cars are you really excited to drive? Which colors speak to you? Which car had the coolest infotainment system? Using your gut, pick the two specific cars (e.g., the 2018 green RAV-4 from dealer #1 and the blue CRV from dealer #2) that bubble to the top of the list. Test drive those two specific cars and choose the one that you like the best. If you are buying directly from another person, bring the car to a mechanic to make sure that it is in good shape; if it is from a dealer, this step is not necessary. And now you're done. Congratulations!

This example shows that the decision-making framework needs to be flexible, as there are many different types of decisions. As I said before, feel free to make your own template, adding or subtracting from this one—what matters most is not the specific template you use, but having a template in the first place. Once you have that framework, remember to subject it to a feedback loop to constantly improve its effectiveness. As with anything else, "practice makes easy,"[8] and the more you use a framework to make decisions, the more natural it will become.

Pauses to think in the decision-making process should happen both at the beginning and the end. The first *pause* is when you decide to ignore your snap judgement and enter a full-blown process. The second *pause* is when you are performing the final evaluation, being honest about your likelihood of regretting the decision and your emotional satisfaction with the choice you have made. Each *pause* serves a different purpose, and two pauses are better than one!

7

Learning

t is highly likely that, though you have spent decades in schools actively listening, reading, watching, doing, writing, and solving, you have never thought about how and why the educational material was presented as it was. Unless you attended a school with significant resources, your teachers probably did not modify their approaches to account for the different learning styles of each student in the classroom. And so, you probably didn't take the time to contemplate which teaching methods resonated most or imparted knowledge most effectively, let alone run personal experiments to compare these different strategies.

For most people, discovering *how* they best learn is a self-guided process of trial and error. Many will experiment with taking notes, underlining, and making flashcards, and settle on a preferred approach.[1] In my academic career, I found that rereading material for history class (skimming first, then reading more deeply) was the best way to retain it, while doing practice problems helped me the most in math.

It hopefully won't be controversial to state that learning strategies should ideally vary based on both the learner and the material. The approaches and mindsets that I will discuss here should improve everyone's learning process, though some may work better than others. Like other frameworks in this book, the first step is the most important: *pause to think*! Before learning something, *pause* to consider how best to learn it. And while learning it, *pause* to consider whether that approach is indeed working or whether you should pivot to a new one.

Let's first summarize what is understood about how our brains function:

1. The brain is very good at making quick decisions from visual stimuli—running away from a charging lion, for example.
2. The brain is very poor at making quick decisions about complex situations and uses mental shortcuts (heuristics) to cope with this weakness.
3. The brain has separate areas dedicated to making short-term memories and long-term memories.
4. The brain is constantly "cleaning up" to rid itself of the huge amount of meaningless information it has accumulated. Much of this happens while you are asleep (it is believed).

With these points in mind, let's zoom out a bit and consider some different situations where we want to absorb, interpret, and retain information:

1. Reading a book and remembering specific information—names and dates, vocabulary, etc.
2. Reading a book or listening to a teacher to learn abstract concepts.
3. Hearing and remembering names, locations, lists of items, or other unrelated information.
4. Memorizing the music or words to a song or a part in a play.
5. Recalling formulae as well as the circumstances under which to use those formulae for math or science applications.
6. Remembering and applying varying approaches to solving unstructured problems.
7. Learning physical techniques, processes, and motions for athletics and other pursuits.

As you consider these tasks, hopefully you appreciate both how varied they are and how different they are from the types of learning that were important to our ancestors (and for which our brains evolved). Mostly, we are not recalling the best bushes on which to find a certain edible berry, the location of a cave, the anatomical weaknesses of a predator, or the type of wood that makes the best fire. The modern world makes demands on our brains that are far more complex.

Before you begin to learn something new, it is important to ask and answer the following questions:

What am I trying to learn?
Who can help me learn most efficiently?
Why is it important to learn this material?
When can I schedule sufficient time to learn and retain this information?
Where can I make credible commitments to facilitate the learning process?
How can I learn it most effectively?

I have again incorporated a mnemonic to aid in the retention of these steps. This is one you have probably seen before: Who, What, Where, When, Why, and How. No points for originality here! If you have the time to write the answers to each of these questions down, it will be helpful to frame your process and to aid in assessing its effectiveness over time.

It is important to critically revisit the learning process after a few days to check whether you are effectively understanding, absorbing, and retaining the information. Pretend that you are a manager and your brain is an employee, and you are giving a performance review at regular intervals and offering feedback if the results are unsatisfactory. This is an example of "double loop" learning, as described below, and it represents a major departure from how most people approach learning. I would wager that for all the time you have spent studying, you have spent almost no time evaluating and considering how to make that study time more efficient and effective. While it may seem intuitive to adjust one's approach based on new information, it is rarely done in practice.

I am now going to introduce various approaches to learning and give examples of circumstances where each might be most helpful. However, as with previous recommendations, you should make your own decisions in this regard, as everyone does have different strengths and weaknesses in the learning area. If you are a very strong memorizer, for example, then you probably should keep doing what you are doing, instead of trying to perfect the "memory palace" technique described below. In my case, my memory was more than adequate when I was younger, but I have found myself relying more heavily on active memorization techniques as I have aged.

Here are the techniques and mindsets:

1. *Deliberate practice*: It is better to work intensely on small subsets of material to master them fully than to spend a short amount of time on many different areas.
2. *Focused versus diffuse learning*: In order to learn a specific body of knowledge or skill as quickly as possible, it is important to focus on the task to the exclusion of all else. However, if the learning is more conceptual or multidisciplinary, allowing the mind to wander (and taking frequent breaks to encourage this) engages the subconscious brain to make connections that the active mind cannot.
3. *Active memorization*: You should convert the material to be memorized into a form that is more effectively processed by your brain. Mnemonics, the process of equating written knowledge with audio or visual identifiers, and "memory palaces" are examples of this.
4. *Checklists*: We have seen these before! Since we are all overconfident, it is best to remember our limits. While performing an activity that requires many discrete tasks, it is important to have a checklist so that none of the tasks are forgotten.

5. *Effective reading and note-taking*: Reading a book cover to cover and summarizing it in outline form, the most common approaches taken by students, are highly inefficient and are probably the largest wastes of time in the educational process.[2]

6. *Double loops*: This method of learning uses feedback from results to change the decision-making process. I already mentioned that this should be your general approach to all learning, but it can also be utilized for certain discrete tasks.

7. *Problem-solving*: If you google "approaches to problem solving," you will find websites touting two-, three-, four-, five-, six-, seven-, eight-, or ten-step approaches to solving problems.[3] I describe an effective and flexible approach that incorporates many of these aspects.

8. *Growth mindset*: This is less of a learning method and more of a learning philosophy. Having a "growth mindset" means working under the assumption that intellectual abilities are not fixed, but rather can be improved through work.[4] It also involves being open to using coaches who can help expand one's mindset and growth potential.

9. *The value of failure*: Failure is seen by many as, well, failure. However, it is increasingly common to celebrate failure and to embrace learning and working methods that allow you to "fail fast." The understanding that comes from failure can frequently more than compensate for the pain of the failure itself.

10. *Avoiding bad habits*: *Inverting* once again, you should consider what actions actively harm your learning process. Distraction and procrastination should be minimized, and counterproductive habits should be replaced with positive ones.

Let's now dig into each of these.

DELIBERATE PRACTICE

Bruce Lee once said, "I fear not the man who has practiced 10,000 kicks once, but I fear the man who has practiced one kick 10,000 times." Deliberate practice is the process of focusing on very small aspects of the task at hand and achieving mastery at each of them before moving on to the next. So, instead of playing ten hours of ping pong and returning hundreds of different types of shots, deliberate practice would advocate spending one hour returning the same shot (say, a deep backhand with topspin).

The human brain will take these repeated behaviors and make them into automatic responses—what we might call "muscle memory"—and it is this automaticity that will be a building block of higher levels of performance.

There is a documentary called *Jiro Dreams of Sushi*, where the apprentice sushi maker is forced to make tamagoyaki (omelets) for ten years before they are deemed good enough. That's right, ten years of making omelets—talk about dedication! Malcolm Gladwell's book *Outliers* popularized the concept of "10,000 hours," which attempts to quantify the amount of deliberate practice required to achieve mastery of a subject. Coaching and feedback (through measurement) can be an important part of deliberate practice, since it is frequently difficult to know what needs to be corrected without that assistance.

The main takeaway here is that all practice is not created equal, and if the goal of practicing is true mastery, then the structure of practice matters. A related warning is that since people prefer to feel good about themselves, they will focus their practice time on material that they already know or perform well (and thus, shouldn't be practicing as much) and less on harder material (which they need to practice more). Removing that bias and focusing on that which is more challenging are real benefits to seeing meaningful improvement. Many *bottlenecks* exist solely because resolving them is particularly difficult or unpleasant!

FOCUSED VERSUS DIFFUSE THINKING

Concentrate! No, don't! Actually, it depends on what you are trying to achieve. It is usually assumed that focusing on a topic will lead to a better learning result. The amount of Adderall consumed in this country is testament to this, and for many tasks the assumption does hold true—studying for a test that requires the retention of a certain set of information, for example. However, on many occasions it is better to let the mind wander or take a break from a certain activity and return to it later. It is important to use the appropriate method for a given situation (figure 7.1).

Diffuse thinking works by making connections among different areas of the brain. These connections are formed passively and unconsciously, which is why some recommend thinking about a difficult problem as you fall asleep, then writing down your earliest thoughts upon waking.[5] Focusing too much on a given problem can be counterproductive, as one's brain gets "stuck" on a certain approach or perspective. When solving crossword

Diffuse

➤ Subconscious/unconscious
➤ Mind wanders
➤ Broad and shallow
➤ Untargeted
➤ Strategic
➤ Making connections

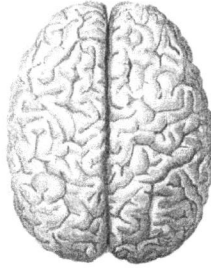

Focused

➤ Conscious
➤ Concentration
➤ Precise and deep
➤ Specific
➤ Tactical
➤ Deliberate practice

FIGURE 7.1 Focused versus diffuse thinking.

puzzles, for example, it is common for me to unsuccessfully ponder one clue for five minutes, put down the puzzle for a few hours, and then return to the crossword and complete it almost immediately.[6]

Think about that for a second. You spent five frustrating minutes trying to solve the clue "One getting fired up for competition." You set down the crossword, convinced that the clue is too hard to answer. Then you return to the puzzle at a later hour, having spent no time thinking about the clue. You look at it, and the answer ("starter pistol") immediately jumps into your mind. Your brain was still processing that information in the background so that it would be ready for you when you needed it. Kind of crazy, right? But in a good way! And it's not just crossword puzzles, of course. At least one book has been written about harnessing the power of your unconscious mind in a variety of settings, replete with quotations from numerous Nobel Prize winners crediting this approach for contributing to their intellectual discoveries.[7]

Conversely, focused thinking, at its best, allows you to enter a state of "flow." This is a somewhat meditative state where you are entirely focused on one activity or thought without distraction, which allows you to achieve a level of mastery or understanding not otherwise attainable. Even without activating this level of focus, careful concentration can be used to cement discrete knowledge. And as discussed by many learning experts, this intense focus can lead to exceptionally rapid skill acquisition.[8]

Many broad areas of learning require both types of thinking, depending on the part of the task that is being learned. Table 7.1 shows some examples of situations in which you will want to use each approach, depending on the topic.

Table 7.1 Appropriate topics for focused and diffuse thinking

Focused	Diffuse
Math multiplication	Mathematical proofs
SAT verbal multiple choice	SAT verbal essay portion
KenKen	Crossword
Soccer penalty shots	Soccer dribbling
Spanish grammar	Spanish conversation

Before starting to learn anything, *pause* to consider which aspects would benefit from focused or diffuse approaches, and tailor your learning style appropriately.

ACTIVE MEMORIZATION

The structure of memory formation, as cognitive scientists understand it best, is as follows:

— A stimulus is perceived (visual, auditory, tactile, etc.).
— This experience is moved into short-term memory (which lasts ~20 seconds unless it is consciously retained).
— If retained, it is then moved into long-term memory.

Retaining information in the long-term area is the most common definition of "memory." So, how do we do this more effectively? We need to actively instruct our brains which information we want to retain and then make it easy for our brains to process it. Since the brain only retains a tiny percentage of the stimuli it receives, its default action is to erase anything that it isn't specifically asked to keep.

The primary technique for improving memory retention relies on the fact that the human brain is excellent at remembering visual information, especially that which is notably different from other images seen before. This is directly related to our evolutionary need to recall fertile hunting grounds or varieties of edible fruit. Our brains are not particularly good at remembering numerical values or written information, so we must associate these with stories, images, or other mnemonics to retain them effectively. Memories are more easily made when we translate written information into a visual or auditory form.

There are a variety of methods to accomplish this goal:

1. Mnemonics make lists of information into coherent sentences. So, map directions are "**N**ever **E**at **S**hredded **W**heat" (North/East/South/West), while the lines of the treble clef are "**E**very **G**ood **B**oy **D**eserves **F**udge." There are also musical mnemonics (*the ABC song*) and rhyming mnemonics (*30 days hath September*).

2. Flashcards (or apps such as Quizlet) can take a fact and transform it into an image. By isolating one piece of information, actively recalling it, speaking it, and seeing the word written, you are combining many aspects of learning at once. Ideally, the cards have an actual picture on them as well. By subsequently reviewing them on a periodic basis, you are encouraging your brain to move the information from temporary to long-term memory.

3. Creating a mental picture or a video. If you are trying to memorize the first five presidents of the United States, you might picture yourself **Washing** your **Adam's** apple with **Jif** peanut butter on **Madison** Avenue while wearing a **Monocle** (Washington, Adams, Jefferson, Madison, and Monroe). Pretty silly, but that silliness is part of what allows the image to be retained in your mind, as brains retain particularly surprising and nonstandard data. This is a type of story-making process—and remember that the human mind loves *narratives*!

4. A "mind map" transforms a hierarchy of information into a visual, color-coded image.[9] Software makes creating this image a lot easier.

5. A "memory palace," as described below.

The memory palace is perhaps the most powerful method for incorporating mental pictures. This technique, which has been used for thousands of years by those serious about memorization, involves using a familiar physical space to memorize long lists of words, objects, or numbers.

The first step in this technique is to picture an environment that you know intimately and can easily picture in your mind. Commonly, this is your bedroom or a larger area of your home. Next, choose various focal spots in the room, starting from the entry doorway and proceeding clockwise around it. So, the door might be Point 1, a picture on the wall is Point 2, a corner bookshelf is Point 3, a desk is Point 4, and so on. It is into these slots that you place mental pictures as described earlier—incongruous images that use outrageous juxtaposition to stick in your memory.

For example, if you wanted to memorize the ten countries with the highest populations, you might put a model of the Taj Mahal, in fluorescent pink, representing India in the first slot (the doorway). In the picture frame (point 2) you could put a massive dumpling filling the entire space, representing China, and so on. Then imagine yourself walking through the room, taking in each of these bizarre objects. If possible, animate them (for example, have them yell something mean or funny at you), since this also helps to make the images more memorable.

You can also use this technique to memorize long lists of numbers, once you associate various sounds of consonants with the numbers one through ten, and various other approaches to remember different types of lists. If you have any doubts about this approach, know that it is the preferred technique for memory champions, who can perform incredible feats of memorization, such as reciting the first 70,000 digits of Pi. As such, it is worth taking seriously and potentially making part of your learning repertoire.

CHECKLISTS

A checklist is just as it sounds—a list of tasks or considerations that you consult to ensure that none are inadvertently overlooked. It is as simple and boring as you imagine. And yet, it is surprisingly powerful.

Remembering a long list of tasks or objects can be quite difficult, as the human mind is not designed for this type of thinking. Of course, you could develop a memory palace to retain this information, but most people don't (until they read this book, that is!). As a result, people frequently forget parts of long lists. Surgeons forget steps in their operating procedure. Investors forget to assess certain financial ratios. Airplane pilots forget to perform some safety checks. All these workers, and many more, have been helped by using checklists.

In one analysis, surgical checklists led to a 50 percent decline in the surgical death rate.[10] Planes would crash regularly due to pilot error before the U.S. Air Force introduced checklists in the 1940s; now they rarely do. Well-regarded investors of all types use checklists to improve their research process.[11]

So, when you need to remember a long list of items or actions, use a checklist (or a checklist app). There is no shame in writing them down, and the benefit received from using this simple tool will be well worth the effort.

EFFECTIVE READING AND NOTE-TAKING

These are the building blocks of knowledge acquisition, and you are probably doing them all wrong! Reading can be made more effective by skimming over less relevant sections, starting your reading at the end of chapters to absorb the conclusion first, and interrupting your reading to actively consider the material. The note-taking approach should vary based on the goal of those notes (e.g., for active learning, future review, to supplement presentation slides, or as preparation for future writing). While these skills were likely most important as you went through high school and college, the reality is that reading is a lifelong pursuit, while taking notes is vital to retaining the information that you read and hear every day in the business world.

As always, there are dozens of books and articles on these topics, and I will only offer a few recommendations. Remember to experiment with the ways in which you read and summarize that information and change your methods when they aren't working. Here is a general framework that I find useful and is grounded in several different proven methods:

1. Be explicit about why you are reading the material. Is there specific knowledge you are hoping to obtain (such as evidence to use in a paper or presentation), or is this part of an open-ended research process? Keep this broader goal in mind as you read.
2. Find the central thesis of the book or article from the introductory chapter or paragraph, or an online summary or review. Write it down, ideally in an app or online document that allows you to edit easily.
3. Identify the supporting points from the index, the chapter introductions, or the end-of-chapter summaries that authors provide. Write those down as well.
4. Give yourself no more than an hour to skim the material. Write down anything that you find interesting (quotations, ideas, or related readings), regardless of whether it directly supports the main thesis.
5. Review your notes once and then walk away for a few days. In this time, your "diffuse learning" mechanisms will process the information.
6. After this time, decide whether the material is worth further exploration. Not all books are good, and many won't merit your time (remember *opportunity cost*). It is likely that the process outlined above will be adequate for most educational purposes. So, if you decide to stop here, review your notes once more, and then move on.

7. If you want to dive deeper (since you enjoy the material or find it particularly helpful), go back and start reading from cover to cover. Read with a purpose (as defined in Step 1) and write down information that pertains specifically to that purpose. Reexamine the need to keep reading the book every few hours and stop if the *marginal utility* is dropping too low.

For taking notes, there are a variety of approaches that can be employed, including the Cornell method, mental maps, and apps such as Evernote. None of these are clearly better than the others, and as long as you are matching the notes themselves to the purpose of the reading, the outline in which those notes are contained is simply a matter of personal preference. Look through some of the resources at the end of the book for some online discussion and reviews.

DOUBLE LOOPS

Double loop learning is an approach that not only corrects errors but also improves the assumptions inherent in the learning process. If you are learning how to play the piano, for example, single loop learning would tell you to keep working on a certain fingering sequence until you played all the notes correctly. Double loop learning would add to this the question of whether that fingering pattern is optimal for the piece or if instead you should try a different one.

Double loops are an important aspect of machine learning and artificial intelligence, which rely on computers continuously examining data for patterns, hypothesizing relationships among the data, testing the model that results, and then further improving the model from the conclusions of that process. Artificial intelligence is kind of a big deal these days, so why not borrow from one of its primary techniques?

The basic assumption here is that your approach to learning should evolve, and that any given process should be flexible. Of course, it is important to learn efficiently using the methods and approaches that you have been taught. Frequently, these are approaches that have been employed for many decades and found to be most effective. However, this does not mean that these approaches cannot be improved upon, or that an approach that works well for most people will work just as well for you. In fact, it is increasingly the case that students are found to have different optimal learning styles—auditory, visual, textual, physical, and social—and thus may more effectively retain information if it is presented differently.

So, if you find that your learning progress is not satisfactory when using a method that has been proposed by a teacher or a textbook, try a different approach to see if it is more effective. Watch a YouTube video or draw a picture, set the information to music, or even write a poem. *Pause to think* about your learning outcomes and refine the process if you find them lacking. In the words of Steve Jobs, think different![12]

PROBLEM-SOLVING

So far, I have focused on learning material that has a defined scope and pre-established processes. When handed a new problem, you don't always have this luxury and instead must work in an unstructured format.

Problem-solving is a bit like Frogger, for those of you who remember the classic arcade game. You can move forward, move backward, or move from side to side to open up new potential paths. Solving a problem or reaching a goal is akin to moving forward, understanding the root causes of a problem is akin to moving backward, and experimenting with different approaches is the lateral change. Each step involves a phase of brainstorming and a phase of analysis and deductive reasoning.

If you determine that you have a problem you are trying to resolve, start by moving backward and performing a root cause analysis. This involves stating the problem and questioning why it exists, on an iterative basis. In the Six Sigma lean production approach (used by many of the world's most efficient manufacturing companies), they are taught to ask "why" no fewer than five times, which seems like a reasonable rule of thumb (figure 7.2).

Feel free to consult your checklist of biases and concepts, as some may show up as root causes. *Incentives, sunk costs, bottlenecks, activation energy*, and *causation* seem particularly salient here.

If the problem involves a goal instead of a cause, then just change "why" to "how" and work forward (*invert* the root cause analysis) (figure 7.3).

Once you finish this part of the analysis, try to identify which causes or steps toward a goal are likely to have the most impact, using the *80/20 rule*. There are three main approaches to generating solutions for these problems, and they should all be used in parallel.

Problem: Consumers aren't buying our product   **Why?**

1. It's too expensive   **Why?**
    a. Our supplier raised prices   **Why?**
        i. Raw material inflation   **Why?**
            ▪ COVID
            ▪ Mine accident in Malaysia
        ii. Logistics costs   **Why?**
            ▪ Ocean freight shortage
        iii. Single sourced   **Why?**
    b. The quality is much higher than competitors' products
    c. Low turnover means retailers need a large markup
        i. We haven't spent any money on in-store promos
2. It's not being marketed effectively   **Why?**
    a. TV ads ate up the marketing budget   **Why?**
        i. Our marketing guy came from a TV background
    b. We are trying to grow into new areas   **Why?**
        i. Board made this a strategic imperative
            ▪ Our core market isn't growing
3. Distributors don't want to carry it   **Why?**
    a. It's not profitable given the low inventory turns

FIGURE 7.2 Root cause analysis of consumer product sales.

1. *Brainstorming*: Think of as many potential solutions as possible, as broadly and creatively as you can. You should embrace both *focused* and *diffuse* thinking and alternate their application. The mantra of brainstorming is "no bad ideas," so generate as many as you can!
2. *Research*: Look into how others have solved similar problems by reading books and articles and speaking with others, and consider whether their solutions are applicable. Embrace both the *internal* (surveys, interviews) and *external* (data analysis of a wide set of similar problems) approaches— use different *perspectives*.
3. *Analysis/deduction*: Use logic to divide the problem into smaller steps and then make reasonable assertions about how to progress to each step. *Deductive reasoning* and *game theory* come in handy here.

Goal: I need to save $25,000 for a down payment on a house   **How?**

1. Earn more money   **How?**
   a. Get a new job   **How?**
   b. Ask for a raise at my current job   **How?**
   c. Find a side hustle   **How?**
2. Spend less money   **How?**
   a. Don't go out to eat   **How?**
      i. Learn to cook!   **How?**
   b. Move in with my parents   **How?**
      i. Convert the basement into a bedroom
   c. Cancel vacation   **How?**
   d. Pay off credit card debt   **How?**
3. Monetize assets   **How?**
   a. Sell car and take the bus   **How?**
      i. Call dealers to solicit bids
      ii. Put an ad on Craig's List
   b. Sell baseball card collection   **How?**
      i. Put it on eBay
      ii. Take it to a collectibles shop

FIGURE 7.3 Inverted root cause analysis of saving for a down payment.

Some potential ideas for the first example might be:

– Can we diversify suppliers?
– Should we rebid our logistics contracts?
– Can we reengineer the product to cost less without significantly reducing quality?
– Can we provide incentives to distributors or retailers to carry and promote the product?
– Should we sell the product directly through our own website?
– Should we engage a marketing consulting firm to explore new media?
– Can we determine whether new markets are likely to be profitable and exit them if not?

For the second we might ask:

— Do any of my friends know of interesting jobs at their companies?
— Are there listings on LinkedIn or other job sites that are worth perusing?
— How much money would I save if I learned to cook?
— Will my parents let me move in with them?
— Are there viable alternatives to owning a car?
— Can I put a few baseball cards on eBay and see how well they sell?

Now, depending on the time and resources at your disposal, as well as the confidence you have in any given approach, you can implement one or more potential solutions to the problem. Using multiple lines of attack (an "experimental" approach) is almost always better if you can implement them, and companies do this all the time through A/B testing. If you are confident in a single analytical/deductive solution, try that first. In either case though, remember to regularly analyze the success of the solution so that you can alter it if needed, incorporating a double loop learning approach.

GROWTH MINDSET

Having a growth mindset means that a learner views their capacity for learning as unbounded. Intelligence is not fixed, as aptitude tests might suggest, but rather dynamic and expandable. This optimistic attitude makes a huge difference in how learners approach their educational experience.

A fixed mindset learner will view a setback as an indication of their lack of ability, whereas a learner with a growth mindset will view it as an opportunity to improve their intelligence. The explanation for this is simple—if you believe that your intelligence is fixed and you fail at a task, then this failure represents an inherent inability to perform. This cannot be changed by hard work, as it is genetically predetermined. So, when confronted with failure, your optimal response is to stop trying![13]

This framework was scientifically reasonable as of a few decades ago, when most research showed that mature brains did not develop new neurons and new neural pathways did not form after a certain age. However, recent research has shown just the opposite—brains can regenerate cells, and new neural connections can be made. This does not mean that the process is simple or easy, but it is possible.

A growth mindset acknowledges this fact. If a learner assumes that their capacity is unbounded, they will view failure as a minor setback and hopefully even as an opportunity to learn and improve. A virtuous cycle (aka a *positive feedback loop*) will then ensue—belief in one's ability to grow will be the motivation to try harder, which will provide evidence of improvement and achievement, further validating the original belief.

THE VALUE OF FAILURE

Closely tied to the growth mindset is the embrace of failure as a learning tool. I would go so far as to say that in many situations, failure is not only unavoidable but desirable, for only by failing will we learn lessons important enough to achieve real progress. However, since many cognitive biases exist so that people can feel good about themselves, failure is rarely viewed in the positive light it deserves.

We can go back to Thomas Edison, who finally found a working filament for an incandescent lightbulb after more than 10,000 attempts proved unsuccessful. Just before that discovery he stated that "I have not failed. I've just found 10,000 ways that won't work." Creative and engineering processes frequently require trial and error; it is not appropriate to label these trials as failures, as they provide information that helps get closer to the right answer. James Dyson, the British engineer who revolutionized the vacuum cleaner (among other household appliances), made 5,127 prototypes over fifteen years before finding a successful approach. He probably learned something from each of those "failed" prototypes!

It is not only mechanical engineers that find value in failure. When Google employees fail at a new project, they throw a party![14] Failure is celebrated, as it encourages employees to take risks that they otherwise might not if failure were punished. Additionally, Google (and much of Silicon Valley) believes in the benefit of "failing fast and failing often"—if you are going to fail, you may as well do so quickly (and own it—looking at you, Elizabeth Holmes) instead of hiding the fact and consuming valuable time and resources in the process. Put another way, as Bill Gates said, "Success is a lousy teacher."

In scientific research, failure is rarely celebrated—after all, who wants to spend several years researching a certain hypothesis only to find that it is incorrect? But there is real value in this failure, as it informs the future research paths of other scientists and adds to the collective repository of information. Consider the following thought experiment: say that one million students are considering dedicating their lives to cancer research. They magically know ahead of time (through the powers of *probability* and *statistics*) that only one of them will discover a miracle cure, and the rest of them will fail in their efforts. Of course, it is impossible to predict which path of investigation will lead to a cure for cancer ahead of time (*ex-ante*, as some might say). Should these students still pursue this career?

I hope they all do, for the good of all humanity! Embracing failure and professional careers that have a high risk of failure is necessary for the important goal of advancing human knowledge. But to do so, people in those areas will have to acknowledge that failure really isn't so bad, lest they go through life with permanent frowns on their faces.

AVOIDING BAD HABITS

Since many of these approaches require some discipline to implement, it is important to have techniques in place that will help you offset your natural counterproductive tendencies. *Inverting* our discussion, we can see that improving our learning processes requires removing that which hinders them. The main barriers to effective learning are procrastination, distraction, and poor habit formation.

Procrastination is learning's public enemy number one! Research shows that the most effective way to acquire and retain information is to stretch it out over a long period of time and reinforce it regularly ("spaced repetition"). This is why earlier discussions around reading and flashcards recommended taking time between study sessions. Conversely, cramming the night before is nearly useless for long-term knowledge acquisition, yet the only approach possible after too much delay. So, avoiding procrastination is a key part of effective learning, and the best ways to do this seem to be:

1. *Develop a reasonable plan*: Set a schedule that is feasible based on the other demands on your time. Make sure that it is consistent but not overwhelming and use smaller sessions with breaks in between (this is called the Pomodoro Technique if you want to google it). During the breaks, allow yourself to engage in the activities that you usually use to procrastinate (social media, texting, video games, etc.), but in limited amounts.

2. *Give yourself the proper incentives*: To keep the end goal in sight and in mind, remind yourself of why you are learning the material. Have positive

incentives ("If I ace the test, I can buy myself those new sneakers") to infuse the necessary *activation energy* while also employing negative *incentive structures* ("I will Venmo $20 to my friend, which she will only return to me if I prove that I studied 30 minutes today"). These negative incentives are also called "credible commitments," a term from *game theory*, where you are forcibly imposing a restrictive, explicit, and yet beneficial structure upon yourself.

3. *Find a study partner*: Having a study partner not only motivates you to study (using your cognitive biases such as *reciprocity* to your advantage), but actively discussing the material (known as "active recall") as you are studying helps cement it in your mind.

Distraction is procrastination's partner in crime. Who among us hasn't felt our eyes stray away from our book and toward the warm embrace of our smartphone, with its delectable offerings of social media, texts, and music? For our brain to process and retain the material that is entering through the visual cortex, though, it must stay focused. And so, you should:

1. Put your phone in a different room, turn it off, or (at the very least) enable its silent mode.
2. Turn off Spotify unless you are listening to classical music or ambient sounds.
3. Create a dedicated study space that is free of screens, pictures, games, outdoor vistas, or other items that compete for your mind's attention.
4. Avoid multitasking and focus on one topic at a time for the whole learning session. Remember to practice deliberately.

Developing good learning habits is no different than acquiring other beneficial habits, and so it is worth reviewing some principles in that area as well. The most modern habit acquisition framework seems to be that put forth by James Clear in his book *Atomic Habits*. The book also highlights the power of small improvements to produce significant results (borrowing from the idea of *compound interest*), but we will only discuss his habit-forming technique here. He suggests four steps:

1. *Make it obvious*: Explicitly state what habit you are trying to form, and why.
2. *Make it attractive*: Attach *incentives* to the habit acquisition or join a group that is pursuing the same goal.

3. *Make it easy*: Reduce friction in the process, optimize your environment (by removing distractions), and make credible commitments.

4. *Make it satisfying*: Employ a *double loop* approach to evaluate your progress and add positive or negative *incentives* along the way.

It is no coincidence that Clear's framework borrows many concepts that we have already reviewed—he is a big fan of mental models! And of course, developing positive habits is, at its core, the imposition of a "slow thinking" process onto a "fast thinking" one, replacing our self-destructive instinctive behavior with reason-derived goals.

CONCLUSION

Hopefully this chapter provides you with some perspectives on different learning methods and approaches. Remember that the process of learning how you best learn is itself a learning process. That sentence was so convoluted that you might even remember it (since you probably had to re-read it a few times!) Remember also to assume that there is always room for experimentation and improvement in your learning approach. And of course, remember to *pause* and ask yourself Who, What, Where, When, Why, and How before and during the process.

8

Understanding

UNDERSTANDING

T he goal of this chapter is to improve your intellectual defense as well as your offense. Just as you have trained your mind to be aware of certain biases, you need to be on the lookout for when other people are intentionally exploiting these biases to unduly influence you. Knowing these tricks will allow you to outsmart these attempts and avoid falling prey to falsehoods.

Advertising and fake news are similar in that both manipulate us into actions we might not have taken without them. Advertisements generally won't contain outright lies due to legal consequences, but they will leave out salient details or intensely focus on one aspect while ignoring others. Fake news can be largely fabricated but have a kernel of truth mixed in to add credibility, all of which is protected by our laws of free speech. This is clearly more sinister, but both share a common intent to deceive. This is what we must work hard to immunize ourselves against.

One would hope that scientific journals endeavor to be as accurate as possible and would only promote papers written by ethical researchers and reviewed by competent peers. However, as we will see, there are many biases at work here as well. The field is brutally competitive, and these pressures occasionally result in scientists publishing falsified results. Even those that are not faked may not be reproducible, indicating that the results were based on chance. The main way to deceive in these papers is using statistics, and through a proper understanding of statistical methods, you will be able to hold informed opinions on the accuracy and significance of the conclusions that are reached.

It goes without saying (at this point) that you should *pause to think* about the context of the information, the motivations of the authors, and the potential ways in which misrepresentations could occur. Don't be afraid of applying a healthy dose of skepticism, as the technological and psychological tricks grow ever more sophisticated.

ADVERTISING

It should come as no surprise that advertising techniques are designed to appeal to many known cognitive biases. We have already discussed the use of *reciprocity* by not-for-profit organizations, such as when they send you a "free" tote bag and then solicit a donation. *Social proof* is another commonly used approach, as advertisers convince you that you will be in good company if you use their product (e.g., using celebrity endorsers). Humans' willingness to listen to authority is another trait that is expropriated by the advertising industry, with doctors being frequent spokespeople. The use of public relations, also known as "unpaid advertising," allows advertisers to have "legitimate" media (such as newspapers) publish or televise stories about the company or one of its products, which confers legitimacy.

However, another common technique is to use poor statistical techniques to persuade you that a certain conclusion is valid. Here are some examples—hopefully you haven't been fooled by them!

1. A restaurant advertises that they have the "#1 Hamburger in the City, as voted by our customers!"
   Of course, if someone goes to a certain restaurant for their burgers, they must like those burgers! This is a good example of *sample selection bias*. I have been voted World's #1 Father by my children, though I'm pretty sure there was no bias involved in that particular award.
2. "Four out of five dentists recommend Colgate!"
   The telephone survey allowed multiple choices, so it is more accurate to state that "four out of five dentists recommend Crest, Colgate, or some other brand of toothpaste."[1] I guess the fifth dentist preferred to brush without any toothpaste. Additionally, this type of advertising was historically used for more pernicious recommendations, such as the advertising campaign from 1946 that stated, "More doctors smoke Camels than any other cigarette!"
3. "50 percent off!"
   This seems like a nice discount, unless the company has doubled the list price before applying the reduction, as they likely did! This is an example of *anchoring*, where customers are anchored at the higher price printed on the ticket, and so consider the discount a bargain.
4. "I'm not only the Hair Club president, I'm also a client."[2]
   This Hair Club for Men advertising campaign from 1986 featured its founder making this statement. People love *narratives* and are drawn to stories from customers. This is why commercials feature "real customers" talking about their experiences, and even the statement that they are paid for their endorsements doesn't seem to diminish the power of their statements.

There are numerous other examples of advertisers' tricks. Instagram influencers take advantage of *social proof*, where people like to be surrounded by others doing the same thing as they are. Subscriptions with

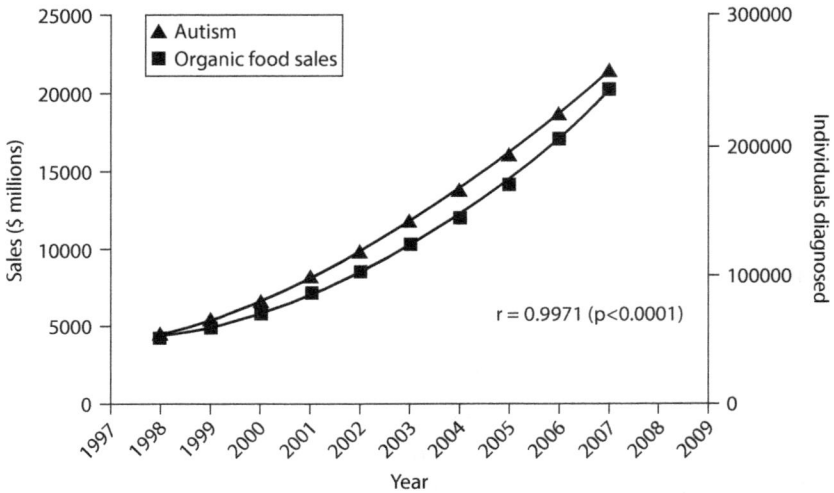

FIGURE 8.1 Spurious correlation. Graph by u/jasonp55 on Reddit, https://imgur.com /1WZ6h.

free trials play both to the concept of the endowment effect (you don't want to give up what you already have) and the tendency to stick with the status quo. And of course, all advertising is an exercise in *framing*—giving the best possible presentation of a product and highlighting its benefits while ignoring its drawbacks.

Moreover, random chance (or a poorly designed scientific study) can give the impression of *causation* when none exists. Figure 8.1, which casts doubt on the hypothesized relationship between vaccinations and autism, reflects this spurious correlation.[3]

Of course, the easiest way to sell products is just to make up false benefits, as many weight-loss companies seem to do. Here are just a few examples of unscrupulous people, caught in the act:

Ad Agency to Pay $2 Million for Role in Deceptive Weight Loss and "Free" Offers[4]
Caught on Video: Can Herbalife Cure a Brain Tumor?[5]
ExtenZe Herbal Nutritional Supplement[6]

If the statement comes from a reputable company (which listens to its lawyers) you can look for the asterisk at the end of the claim. If a battery brand "lasts longer," look at the battery to which it is being compared and decide if that is the right comparison. Recently, when Tesla's pickup truck was shown winning a tug of war with a Ford F-150,[7] it was reasonable to ask which engine and transmission were being used in the contest.

Finally, don't forget that all humans want to show you the best version of themselves, and this holds especially true if they are trying to profit from the encounter. Airbrushing, cropped photos, and fake models are commonplace, especially for consumer products.[8]

In a recent article, teenagers were explicitly made aware of the advertising techniques being used to increase their cravings for unhealthy fast food.[9] Once they were aware of this and channeled their appropriate indignation about being manipulated, they made healthier food choices. Hopefully you will feel similarly after reading this chapter. Just remember to *pause to think* whether advertising claims are reasonable, which of your cognitive biases are being targeted, and (most importantly) whether you really need to buy that product!

FAKE NEWS

The book *How We Know What Isn't So* by Thomas Gilovich discusses how some of the cognitive biases discussed earlier can lead people to hold incorrect beliefs.[10] In it, he posits the following, much of which should seem familiar to you at this point:

1. Humans are prone to see patterns where none exist.
2. Humans accept information that confirms previously held beliefs and ignore information that does not.
3. People believe, within limits, what they want to believe.
4. People like stories, and so are comfortable with media stretching the truth (as the *National Enquirer* does), if it is entertaining.

This is a book that was written thirty years ago and yet has special relevance today. That is because the presence of "fake news," behavioral targeting, and a general disregard for truth have become an epidemic. People seem to hold erroneous beliefs more commonly (e.g., autism-causing vaccines, vitamin supplement panaceas, and contrails[11]) and are very comfortable doing so. Perhaps we shouldn't be surprised, though. As Jonathan

Rausch wrote in *The Constitution of Knowledge*, humans have been misrepresenting truth for millennia, with others around them content to support these fake beliefs as long as it serves their own purposes. While it is pleasant to think of humans as primarily rational and truth-seeking, in fact "reason is . . . the slave of the passions," as philosopher David Hume wrote in 1739.

Knowing this predisposition, we must still embrace Daniel Patrick Moynihan's precept: "Everyone is entitled to his own opinion, but not to his own facts." When false information is disseminated alongside facts and done so in a way that targets human biases and inclinations, then readers must be especially wary.

With the progression of technology, it will soon be possible to alter video and audio ("deep fakes") so that any person can appear to say or do anything.[12] Soon, it will be literally impossible to trust your own senses, which is why you must learn to trust your mind.

So let us consider the ways in which fake news is likely to appeal to our preconceptions and biases, and work to build up defenses against these attacks.

1. *Consider the source.* This seems obvious, though sometimes it is not easy to ascertain the true source of the information or the various filters that have been applied (who published it, who wrote it, was the article altered or selectively quoted in some way, etc.). Nonetheless, it is vital to never simply accept a statement as true without considering, however briefly, the *incentives* of those who are making it. Remember the concept of *perspective* and apply it to current events.

2. *Trust facts but distrust projections.* People can be paid to make "informed" projections that support any viewpoint—look at the diversity of opinion around global warming, financial markets, and the health impact of various foods and supplements. Historical facts, when properly compiled and cited, are far more trustworthy than arbitrary opinions about the future, which suffer from the introduction of many cognitive biases.

3. *Disregard narratives.* Knowing that influencers will employ stories, especially those that appeal to our preconceptions, we must be particularly alert when presented with a compelling *narrative*. Demand data or primary evidence, instead of interviews or conjecture.

4. *Check any suspicious images* for signs of editing or tampering, using reverse search tools.[13] More generally, assume that photos can be cropped in many ways,[14] and increasingly, partially or wholly fabricated.

5. *Check the source of any quotation* (using Google Advanced Search), as it could easily have been re-quoted only partially or out of context. Removing parts of a quotation that provide a contrary or nuanced interpretation is entirely consistent with the presence of *confirmation bias* and the avoidance of *cognitive dissonance.*

6. *Look for multiple verifications of data.* If information is cited in many places or linked to by reputable publications or scientific papers, it is far more likely to be legitimate.

7. *Verify expertise.* People naturally defer to experts (*authority bias*) and accept their statements as fact. However, many "experts" are no such thing, and their background and credentials should be verified as both legitimate and relevant to the subject on which they are opining.

8. *Remember that data can be manipulated.* Since most people are inherently uncomfortable with data, they prefer having it interpreted, simplified, and presented to them. However, this introduces the risk that the data are being misused or selectively disseminated. Examine the data collection, study design, and data interpretation methods to ensure that they are not biased.

Finally, it helps that there are professionals who are dedicated to exposing questionable information. Snopes.com, Politifact.com, and Fact-check.org are just a few of the websites that are useful in this regard.

Ultimately, there should be a linear relationship between how surprising a news report or claim is and how much evidence is required to support it. A story that foreign powers are interfering in our elections should not shock anyone, as governments have a long history of doing exactly that. A report that thousands of voting precincts are involved in a massive conspiracy is far more unlikely and should require a large body of evidence to substantiate it.

As evidence grows more and more difficult to trust, it will become more important than ever to rely on the tools discussed in this section. It is possible that as you read this book, the internet is being deluged with false information, doctored images, and deep fake videos spawned from ChatGPT and other AI engines. Remember to *pause to think* about the incentives involved, understand which cognitive biases are being exploited, and examine statistical documentation wherever possible.

SCIENTIFIC RESEARCH

There is a pretty good chance that you are not a scientist, as statistically scientists account for under one tenth of one percent of the world's population.[15] Still, it is a near certainty that you will encounter scientific (or quasi-scientific) information in your life and be required to form an opinion about its accuracy and relevance.

When you read that global warming is not real or that eating Oreos will help you lose weight, you may be naturally skeptical.[16] However, there is likely some scientific "study" presenting "evidence" to which supporters will point. Unless Paula Poundstone[17] or an internet sleuth[18] has already opined, then you will have to draw your own conclusions about the data in question. To do this, you need to be equipped with some basic tools of the trade.

While most scientists are well-meaning and ethical people, not all are. The practice of scientific research is a high-pressure, unrelenting grind, with very high reputational and monetary stakes. If one data point meant the difference between a favorable and unfavorable conclusion, which in turn led to millions of dollars of research grants and gaining tenure, wouldn't you feel pressured to ignore that single piece of bad data? Do you think that others would always do the right thing, especially if they believed, deep down, that their thesis might still be valid and that the negative datapoints could be flukes? Perhaps this dynamic is why up to 35 percent of scientific studies cannot be replicated by other scientists[19] and why photoshopping images seems to occur regularly.[20]

More importantly, scientists are human. They fall prey to the same biases as the rest of us, seeking confirmatory evidence and ignoring that which leads to *cognitive dissonance*. While there are safeguards in place to prevent this—peer reviews, clinical trial design guidelines, statistical analyses—human nature still seeps in. If a trial concludes unfavorably, its results are never publicized, while if it is successful, its results will be presented in the most beneficial light possible.

In an ideal world, your (and my) statistical abilities would be robust enough to understand whether the appropriate indicator of statistical significance is a z-test, a p-test, an f-test, a chi-square test, or one of a dozen others with people's names attached to them (Pearson, Wilcoxon, and Cochran, to name a few). But this is not a reasonable request (I for one have better ways to spend my time), and so we must defer to the experts in this regard. Fortunately, plenty of statistical malfeasance happens during the study design, which we are more easily able to evaluate.

Broadly speaking, a well-designed scientific study will have all the following:

1. A large sample size, ideally hundreds or thousands of subjects.
2. A control group that receives the current standard of care therapy, to set the baseline appropriately. If this is not possible, then giving a placebo to the control group is better than nothing.
3. An unbiased lead investigator, with study costs paid by a disinterested party.
4. A double-blind trial design, so that neither the subjects nor those conducting the trial know who is in each group and thus cannot inject bias into the process.
5. Peer review by a well-regarded journal, ideally one with a high impact factor (the number of times it is cited by other academic papers).[21]

If *any* of these five characteristics is lacking, you should be highly skeptical of the study's conclusions. The study may still have merit, but it is likely to have complicating biases that will be difficult to disentangle, and more data will be needed to have confidence in the results.

When reading scientific papers, keep the following mental models in mind:

1. *Regression to the mean*: There is a reason that it is frequently difficult to reproduce results. Remember that if ten scientists each research a new topic (the effectiveness of genetic testing, say), only the one with the best results will publish them, while the rest will quietly stop their research projects. If the true effectiveness of a genetic test is, say, 90 percent, but there is an element of luck to the process, then the first published paper might show 95 percent effectiveness. Only over time, as more data are released, will the true 90 percent result become apparent.
2. *Statistical significance*: A scientific study requires enough data points to generate statistically significant results. Small sample sizes are unlikely to produce meaningful outcomes unless the results diverge massively from the control group. So, if you see a paper with a small number of data points (say, only ten patients are given a drug), you should assume that luck may have played a role in the reported conclusions, unless the outcomes are dramatic (for example, all ten are immediately cured of a disease).

3. *Framing—using the correct control group*: Most studies use control groups, which represent the outcomes without any intervention (such as how a disease progresses if no drugs are used). However, it is easy to choose an inappropriate or misleading control group to make one's results appear better than they are. By doing this, scientists are framing the situation in the most advantageous manner. If you sense that a control group is strangely selected or that the experiment is being conducted in a non-traditional manner, then there is reason to think that the comparison may be misleading.

4. *The placebo effect*: As discussed in chapter 2, humans report healing even when no "real" medicine is given to them. The human mind induces healing activities in response to the placebo and/or deemphasizes the pain-signaling pathways that are causing discomfort. As such, the right comparison for a drug or procedure is not the absence of the drug, but a placebo. Better yet, a new drug should be compared to the current standard of care.

5. *Causality*: Just as with the advertising discussion above, it is possible to look through datasets and find strong correlations. However, it is not always possible to determine causality from this data, unless the study is properly designed to tease it out. In a recent example, companies are testing people's gut microbiomes (for a fee).[22] But if they find that certain gut bacteria are in the intestines of those with Crohn's disease, they cannot know if the bacteria resulted from the disease or the bacteria caused the disease!

Embracing a healthy amount of cynicism is key here. Even broadly held and well-accepted beliefs, based on historical scientific research, can be totally incorrect. For instance, it is now questionable whether breastfeeding infants is beneficial for children at all.[23] Similarly, in the 1900s, the standard advice was to touch one's baby as infrequently as possible, to avoid "coddling" them,[24] the very opposite of today's attachment parenting movement. If such widely held, scientifically supported conclusions still turned out to be incorrect, what other surprises lie in store?

Bringing this example to current times, we should examine the various claims that were made about COVID-19 medications such as zinc, hydroxychloroquine, and azithromycin at the beginning of the pandemic. The "data" supporting the efficacy of these treatments came from small, poorly controlled studies, where the participants were not chosen randomly. The study "investigators" had significant financial, reputational, and political incentives to report positive results. Unsurprisingly, once examined with the appropriate statistical rigor, these compounds were shown to be worse than useless, likely harming many of those that ingested them.

A recent article in the *New York Times* claimed that emergency room errors were killing 250,000 Americans per year—that's 8 percent of the total deaths in this country each year![25] The methodology behind this research was that one man out of 500 died in a study of Canadian ERs a decade ago, and this percentage (.2 percent) was applied to the annual number of ER visits,[26] which seems like a clear violation of both statistical protocols and common sense. Even the *New York Times* can perform shoddy analysis, it seems.

As always, it is important to *pause* to apply an appropriate dose of skepticism to any claim. Would medicine that reduces inflammation cure a respiratory viral disease? Would hospitals still be in business if inept medical practices in their emergency rooms killed 250,000 people each year? If the government wanted to secretly sterilize its population, would it distribute the chemicals sporadically from small planes' contrails, high up in the atmosphere? Remember cui bono and the discussion of *incentives* and remain cynical!

9

Investing

INVESTING

There are thousands of books on investing, which is unsurprising given how interesting this activity is to people who have disposable income to spend on books. However, most of these are now hopelessly out of date and are more likely to lead you in the wrong direction than on the road to investment success. Fortunately, the concepts we have already covered, along with a bit of common sense, will allow you to have a positive and productive relationship with the investment world. Note that these conclusions are meant for the casual and individual investor, and that should you choose to make investing your profession, you will naturally be expected to learn more sophisticated techniques. That having been said, the recommendations in this chapter will (statistically) outperform most professional investors, with much less work!

In my opinion, the keys to successful investing are as follows:

1. Understand the motivations of those on the other side of the investment—the promoters, financial advisors, investment managers, or stock owners.
2. Remember *margin of safety, risk/reward, mean reversion*, and other salient concepts.
3. Do not fall prey to cognitive biases and behavioral mistakes, such as finding comfort in "the crowd," overreacting to short-term events, or minimizing emotional discord.
4. Embrace statistical and probabilistic methodologies.
5. Remember the power of compound interest and the negative impact of large losses on this process.

This is a general framework, though when most people think of "investing" they naturally think of stocks and bonds first. Investing in equities (stocks) is likely to be the most common and best approach for the vast majority of savers, and as such, I will mostly focus on that area.

WHY FEES ARE BAD

I won't bury the lede here. In general, for efficient markets such as those in developed economies (the U.S., Europe, Japan), *it is almost never worth paying someone to make investment decisions on your behalf.* There is abundant evidence that fund managers, personal financial advisors, and virtually the entire financial apparatus do not justify the exorbitant fees that are charged. There are many resources that show this (including a short, free-to-download book I wrote on the topic[1]), and the continued rise of index-based ETFs demonstrates that many people already appreciate it, so I won't belabor the point.

However, the corollary to this assertion is that individuals should be comfortable and confident investing on their own. A few decades ago, this may have been an incorrect assumption. There was a significant amount of information available to institutional investors that was not accessible by individuals, and it was an expensive and sophisticated undertaking to compete with the professionals. Now, however, the playing field has been mostly leveled. The professionals still hold a small advantage (which is why it doesn't make sense to try to beat them at their own game), but not enough to justify the fees they charge.

This evolution of market structure is incredibly freeing. It means that the assumption of "market efficiency," which was kind of a joke from the time it was conceived back in the 1960s all the way to the early 2000s, is now a reasonable one! This further implies that you can buy stocks at random (with a few constraints), that are likely to do better than both index ETFs and the average over-compensated investment manager. This may sound crazy, but it is true—the data are unequivocal! Let me repeat it: *you will make more money choosing stocks randomly than paying a professional investor to choose them for you.* Further, it is better that you choose stocks randomly instead of ones that you like. As you know from our discussion of cognitive biases, you will tend to like stocks that other investors like as well, and it is thus probable that these stocks are already overpriced relative to their fundamental prospects.

The only bad decision you can make, in fact, is to pay fees—to investment advisors, mutual funds, hedge funds, and even ETF sponsors. Trading fees, investment fees, wrap fees, and really commissions of any sort should be studiously avoided. The amounts may seem reasonable at first, but they add up, and (thinking back to *compound interest*) their negative impact is amplified over time. Even low-fee brokerage accounts, which frequently offer "free" trading, exact their pound of flesh. I have several in my name, and the more I pore over my statements, the more I realize how much of my money they have siphoned off in a variety of highly opaque ways. Anything other than using the "market on close" trading order type, holding cash only in separate online savings accounts (not brokerages), and investing in plain vanilla U.S. stocks is literally giving (a lot of) money away!

WHY PEOPLE CONSISTENTLY MAKE
POOR INVESTMENT DECISIONS

The same biases that lead people to make poor decisions generally will also lead them to make poor decisions in the investment arena. These include:

1. FOMO/social proof
2. Anchoring
3. Confirmation
4. Sunk costs
5. Risk aversion
6. Overconfidence

However, there are also aspects of investing which particularly complicate the decision-making process. The first is what we have discussed about agency problems and asymmetric information. As a passive investor in a mutual fund, you have limited insight into the research, decisions, ethics, and motivations of its manager. Put simply, you just don't know if they are any good at their job (see "The Illusion of Skill," on page 164). Even their historical investment results will usually not be statistically significant unless they span several decades. So, you must decide whether to invest, not invest, or disinvest without sufficient information on which to base your decision. It is basically impossible to make consistently good decisions as a result!

Secondly, it is emotionally challenging to act according to one of investing's most important rules: prospective returns are best when the current situation seems worst, and vice versa. As Nathan Rothschild famously said, "Buy on the sound of cannons, sell on the sound of trumpets"—invest when war is about to start, since other investors are at their most pessimistic, and sell when peace is declared. The relevant datum is not that there is a war—this is well-understood by all market participants. The important point is that wars always end and buying when prices are low due to overall pessimism leads to attractive future returns.

But (and this is a big but) this is easier said than done! Fortunes could have been made in March of 2020 at the height of the COVID-19 pandemic, but most investors instead curled into balls and slowly rocked themselves back and forth. Humans avoid discomfort, and there is very little that is less comfortable (other than reading Elon Musk's tweets) than buying stocks when your friends, family, and television hosts are all screaming about impending doom.

This desire for comfort also leads many to engage the services of investment advisors. These professionals are usually very friendly and moderately intelligent, which makes them quite dangerous to your wallet! Remember that every successful investment advisor started with no clients and has worked hard to build their roster through cold calling, paid leads, and referrals. In other words, they are salespeople at heart and will use *reciprocity* and other cognitive biases to their benefit. Also remember that their *incentives* differ from yours, and that their commitment to fiduciary duty (if it legally exists) varies widely. Even if the fee structure is simple (say, a flat percentage of assets), there are still plenty of ways for the advisor to make more money at your detriment—buying high-fee (and commission) mutual funds, allocating their more lucrative investments into performance-based accounts, or having different fee structures for stocks versus bonds, for example.

In summary, human nature will usually lead you astray in matters of money. To be a truly excellent investor, you must learn to ignore the base urges that will lead you to buy high (to avoid FOMO) and sell low (in a market panic)—this is not a good strategy, if you do the math! However, to be an above-average investor is simple: all you must do is take as few actions as possible. And we again *invert*, since eliminating bad decisions will tend to lead to positive outcomes.

Thus, it is best to employ an investment plan that removes the need and likelihood of counterproductive activity. Suggestions include:

1. Ignoring the value of your investment portfolio for long stretches of time, so that you are not tempted to react to price changes.
2. Setting up automatic savings and investment options, so that most of the decision-making is taken out of your hands completely.
3. Ignoring online and television commentary, broker solicitations, and other unhelpful and conflicted investment advice.
4. Avoid all high-fee investment products so that time works in your favor, not against you.

AN ILLUSTRATION OF COMPOUND INTEREST AND WHY LOSSES HURT SO MUCH

Compound interest, as previously discussed, is the process of earning interest on interest, so that the overall effect is exponential. You may have heard that the island of Manhattan was bought from the Lenape tribe for

Table 9.1 Value of retirement savings over time

Age when savings begins	Value of $1,000 at retirement
20	$90,017
30	$33,115
40	$12,182
50	$4,482

$24 worth of beads in 1626. But did you then bother to calculate that this same $24, invested at 10 percent per year until today, would be worth $650 quadrillion (that's $650 thousand trillion)? The current estimate for the land value of Manhattan is around $2 trillion, so perhaps the sellers got a good price after all!

The magic of compound interest is most obvious over long periods. Referring to table 9.1, you can see that, all else equal, it is highly advantageous to begin saving earlier in life.

Less well understood, though, is the outsized penalty that one bears for losing money. This is because losses need to be compensated for by inverse gains. A 50 percent loss reduces $1,000 to $500, which means that now a 100 percent return is required to return to the original amount of principal. Even more dramatically, a 100 percent loss brings your principal to zero, after which no amount of growth can save your retirement!

The following string of returns (produced by, say, investing in electric vehicle stocks) would feel great . . . until it didn't:

Year 1 through Year 9: +25 percent return/year
Year 10: –90 percent return

Value of $1,000 at the end of Year 9: $7,451
Value of $1,000 at the end of Year 10: $745

In comparison, this set of returns (from say, municipal bonds, which are tax-free bonds issued by cities and states) would induce severe FOMO for the first nine years, until vindication came in the tenth (figure 9.1):

Years 1 through Year 9: +5 percent return/year
Year 10: +5 percent return

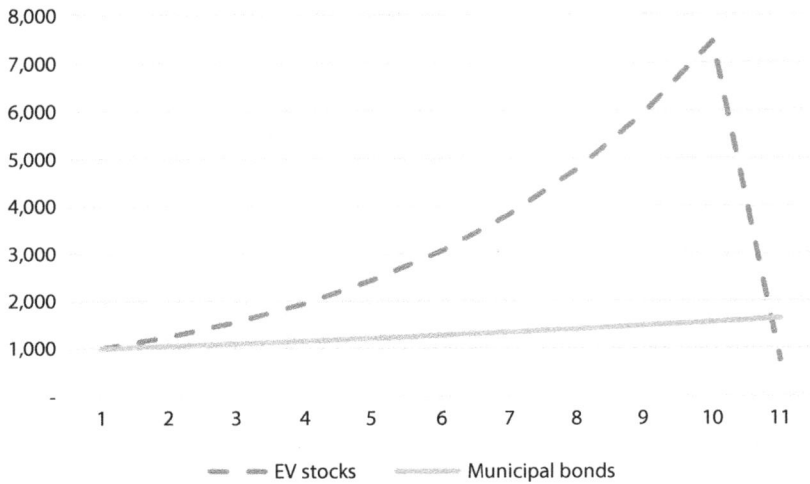

FIGURE 9.1 The deleterious effect of large losses.

Value of $1,000 at the end of Year 9: $1,551
Value of $1,000 at the end of Year 10: $1,628

It takes a very confident person to ignore the transitory riches enjoyed by others as an investment bubble inflates. As in the fable "The Tortoise and the Hare," "slow and steady" eventually wins the race, though it can be an emotionally painful process. In real life, "fast and steady" is the dominant approach, but unfortunately it is vanishingly rare to have both in the world of investing. Bernie Madoff's investors thought they had found that combination, but we all know how that turned out!

THE ILLUSION OF SKILL

If I flip a coin ten times and it lands on heads each time, you might suspect that I am skilled at flipping coins. After all, the chances of this happening randomly are $(\frac{1}{2})^{10}$, or 1 in 1,024. However, what if I told you that there were 20,000 people flipping coins? Wouldn't you expect a few of them (around twenty) to get ten heads in a row? In the same way, if we say that running an investment fund is akin to guessing on the direction of the market each year, one might expect roughly twenty funds to have outstanding long-term records. And yet, those records would have no bearing on the funds' future investment performance, since they were formed by chance.

Let's set up an even more cynical situation. Say that I am an enterprising stockbroker and I want to persuade prospective clients of my investment skill to entice them to open an account with me (remember that investment advisors are salespeople, first and foremost). To do this, I buy an email list with 10,000 names on it and then compose an email saying, "I would like to be your investment advisor, and my first piece of advice would be to buy Ford stock before the earnings report this week." I also write a second email with the exact opposite recommendation—to sell Ford stock. I send the first email to the first 5,000 people on the list and the second email to the next 5,000. Half of those people will have received a poor investment recommendation, and the other half will have made money. The next week, I email the "winners" with a new investment idea; again, half get one recommendation and the other half get the opposite. The next week I am down to 2,500 recipients, then 1,250, 625, 312, 156, 78, 39, and 20. Those twenty recipients will likely believe that I am a genius, having made them money eight weeks in a row, and should be easily persuaded to open an account. While this hypothetical example is somewhat contrived, is it really that different from mutual fund companies launching dozens of different funds with varying strategies, shutting down the ones that perform poorly, and then trumpeting the "five-star performances" of the remaining successes?

People like *narratives*, and the investment business is filled with them. "We bought the stock because we visited the store and saw the new product and just knew it would be a big hit" is a popular one, for instance. But the reality is that these decisions are rarely based on skill, and the process behind these decisions is explanatory, not causal. In other words, it is frequently the case that a great investment leads to a great narrative, not the other way around.

EXPECTATIONS AND EFFICIENT MARKETS

A common mistake when starting to invest is to confuse positive results with ones that exceed expectations. As a rule, the price of a publicly traded investment reflects the combined opinions of thousands of participants and incorporates all possible available information. Thus, if the future of a company appears bright to you, it is very likely to appear bright to most other people, and the stock price already reflects that opinion.

In other words, there is no free lunch here, and you usually cannot buy a great company for a cheap price. As a proxy (imperfect as it may be) for investors' optimism, we look at something called the "price to earnings ratio," or P/E. If a company is valued at $100 million and it is expected to earn $10 million this year, its P/E is 10×. This means that investors expect, on average, the current earnings to persist for 10–15 years (remember the *time value of money*) and are willing to pay for only those earnings. By contrast, if a different firm also had a $100 million value but only $1 million of earnings, its P/E would be 100×. Since investors are generally not willing to wait 100–200 years to be repaid, they must instead expect that $1 million of earnings to grow to $5–10 million before too long. In other words, they have very high expectations for that company and are quite optimistic about its future. They are willing to pay the same price as the first company but only get $1 million of current earnings instead of $10 million, since they expect the future earnings to be much, much higher.

With most of the companies that are popular these days, this exercise is somewhat meaningless, as many do not earn anything and in fact lose quite a bit of money. So, if you listen to Spotify, eat food delivered by DoorDash, or love the idea of driving a Rivian, be aware that other investors are already incredibly optimistic about these companies, despite none of them generating significant economic earnings. Before buying these stocks, remember that their futures are already assumed to be highly successful, and achieving that expectation will not necessarily lead the stock prices to increase.

DIRECT INDEXING

Let's again embrace *inversion* by considering the errors that most investors make and then endeavoring to avoid them. Think of it like playing tennis. If you are matched against a professional, you will need to make very few mistakes and consistently hit winning shots. But if you are playing against a lower-skilled opponent, all you must do is avoid making unforced errors, such as hitting the ball into the net.

The investing mistakes that you should avoid are:

1. Trying to pick individual stocks that will beat the market (and professional investors).
2. Using any structured investment products, including ETFs, but especially more exotic offerings like structured notes.

3. Investing in stocks with high short interest, which are likely to underperform in the overall market.[2]
4. Trading more than a few times a year, except to harvest tax short-term losses.

While ETFs are superior to mutual funds, they still have significant structural defects, since they are not actually designed to maximize performance. Specifically, ETFs:

1. Use market-capitalization weighting, which buys big stocks and sells smaller ones, which is akin to buying high and selling low.
2. Rebalance according to the index that is being tracked (the S&P 500, most commonly), which is essentially a way to give money to hedge funds and other arbitrageurs.
3. Own heavily shorted stocks to make money lending them out to short sellers (and keeping that money for themselves).
4. Charge fees and don't allow for tax-efficient trading of individual positions.

Creating a portfolio of around 40 stocks should outperform an ETF that tracks the S&P 500 by 2–3 percent a year, and this can be done for free through an online brokerage account. Remember to diversify the holdings among different sectors and avoid heavily shorted stocks, but otherwise pick somewhat randomly and roughly match the sector weights of the S&P 500. There are some more suggestions, as well as a list of potential stocks from which to choose, at www.investforfree.org.

As previously mentioned, the top recommendation is to avoid paying fees wherever possible, as these fees will mostly be far too high for the value received (and that value received is itself more likely to be negative than positive!). Otherwise, investing is a set of personal decisions that vary based on risk tolerance, sophistication, and one's financial situation.

– Know your limits (especially paying attention to what you don't know and whether you are likely to be the "sucker" at the table).
– Make investments that seem to have attractive *risk/reward* characteristics.
– Remember that a loss hurts more than a gain, and don't let cognitive biases (especially *social proof* and *reciprocity*) impact your investing process.
– Try to have *compound interest* work in your favor by making investments that can remain untouched for many years, growing in a tax-free manner.

Finally, it is important to be cognizant that the last forty years have been an exceptionally profitable time to own stocks and bonds, as inflation and interest rates have declined steadily over that period. *Recency* and *availability* biases indicate that your *expectations* for future returns are too high as a result. Therefore, it is important to avoid the temptation to take more risk with your investment portfolio to attempt to achieve higher returns!

If a friend is talking about their latest NFT success, a broker is pitching an exciting-sounding stock, or a pop-up ad advises "getting in on the ground floor" at a new company, remember to *pause to think* and apply these principals. Hopefully, this will allow you to avoid these unproductive investments and the economic and emotional pain that comes with them.

10

Happiness

Many of the decisions we make in our life seem broadly geared toward increasing our current or future happiness. How we define the term "happiness" will differ by individual and even entire cultures, but we all seem to share this general goal. And yet, happiness is among the most elusive of all targets.

There are two primary reasons why achieving lasting happiness is so difficult. First, we are generally misguided in our assumptions of what will make us happy, and second, our brain constantly resets the bar to prevent us from feeling satisfied, something called "the hedonic treadmill." The good news is that these are both solvable problems, and the answers lie in the concepts that we have discussed previously.

Let's start with a stereotypical scenario. Karl studied hard his whole life, received good grades in high school, and was admitted into an Ivy League college. He continued to study hard and earn good grades, completing college and then graduate school. He then continued to work hard and earned a good salary, moved into a nice apartment, and bought a nice car. And yet . . . and yet . . . he wasn't happy.

This is a slightly cringe-worthy example, but it touches on some commonly held beliefs about happiness. A partial list of what we think will make us happy is:

— A successful academic career.
— A prestigious job.
— Material possessions.
— Earning as much money as possible.
— Marrying a beautiful person.

And, perhaps not shockingly, the research shows that none of these things, in fact, will make us happy. Instead, what makes us happy, according to recent studies and common sense, are:

— Enjoyable experiences.
— Meaningful relationships.
— A sense of belonging to a community.
— Feeling respected and valued at work.
— Having enough money to feel comfortable, but not so much that worrying about it becomes its own burden.

As such, the best approach to increasing happiness involves first rethinking our goals and priorities, and then constantly recalibrating our brain to appreciate what we have. To do this, we will need to reexamine many widely held assumptions.

WORK

Let's start with our choice of career, as we will likely spend a large part of our time working, and it will be a significant part of our identity for much of our lives. Changing our perspective on work is easier said than done. You may have already heard the story of the businessman and the shepherd, which goes something like this:

> A shepherd is relaxing under a tree when a businessman walks by and asks him why he doesn't work harder. The shepherd asks why he should if he already is content with his situation. The businessman explains that with hard work, he could increase his flock, hire some workers, make more money, build the business, and then eventually retire . . . at which point he could then relax under a tree.

The story is a parable that reminds us that work is a means to an end, and we should always keep that end in mind. Of course, it glosses over very real concerns such as healthcare coverage, retirement savings, and the cost of raising a family, but the point remains salient. The shepherd knew what made him happy and set his priorities accordingly.[1] This is quite different from the pressures that many of us feel to constantly push forward academically and professionally, achieve success in our careers, and use the fruits of this labor to purchase cars, houses, and vacations. Even if we understand these societal norms, we may not appreciate how deeply these *expectations* have permeated our own consciousness.

That said, the life of a shepherd would probably not make us happy either. First, pastoral life is much harder than it looks, with long nights spent searching for wandering lambs. The job likely lacks intellectual stimulation or variety and may require relocation away from family and friends. It's tough to get a good cellular signal in the mountains. But the true reason to doubt that a shepherd enjoys an existence of sublime pleasure is that life is too complicated for this to be true. A job is not intrinsically great or terrible, but rather depends on a variety of factors including your relationships with your coworkers, how fulfilled you are by the work, the amount of travel and other hardships the work entails, and the respect and appreciation shown by your superiors and clients. Some high-paying jobs are great, and some are terrible; the same goes for jobs that do not pay as well.

So, job satisfaction varies significantly even among similar roles, and moreover does so in an unpredictable manner. As you read this today, you may envision that someday you may be a partner at a big law firm, wining and dining your clients and collecting a fat paycheck. You probably are not envisioning the grueling one-hundred-hour work weeks that you will have to endure for a few decades before enjoying this pleasant result. Moreover, you will not just be a lawyer, you will be a lawyer practicing Specialty A at Firm B, working with Partner C for Client D.[2] It is literally impossible to accurately imagine exactly what your working life will entail. Additionally, even if you could perfectly predict that your *current* self would enjoy that job, you have no idea if your *future* self will do so, and we are notoriously bad at predicting our own intellectual and emotional evolutions.

To repeat Homer Simpson's classic line, "The lesson is, never try." I won't put it quite that starkly, but I do think that you should calibrate your expectations appropriately. The odds of finding a wonderful job are not in your favor, and your ability to predict which job that will be (given the number of unknown variables) is also very poor. According to Gallup, under 10 percent of people who are looking for a great job believe that they have one.[3] You may find a job that you love, but consider that a fortunate outcome, not a goal unto itself.

It may be helpful to inject some historical perspective here as well. Only recently has this focus on job satisfaction been so prevalent. Perhaps expectations have been reset by proselytizing internet entrepreneurs who have changed the world while allowing their employees to play beer pong and grow fabulously wealthy at the same time. But for most of human (and pre-human) history, jobs were the part of your day that involved unpleasant toil, the price paid to ensure the survival of you and your family. Some of us are lucky enough to live in a very different world where our expectations are reasonably higher, and work is not so closely tied to survival.[4] But we are not yet so evolved as a society that jobs will be the sources of great joy and satisfaction.

I believe the best we can do is the following:

1. *Invert* the question and rule out jobs that no one enjoys—those that have no human contact, require no original thought, are physically or emotionally punishing (including those with very long commutes, though these may be ameliorated by the recent hybrid work trend), or conflict with your fundamental beliefs.
2. Stay flexible in the development of your work skills such that you can move among different firms and roles until you find a good personal and intellectual fit. Focus on your *comparative advantages* to make sure that your skills are marketable.
3. Remember that work is generally a source of dissatisfaction, and avoid jobs that require extended hours or other clear sacrifices throughout the entire career trajectory. In other words, look for jobs that have *declining marginal costs* and *increasing marginal benefits* as your experience increases.
4. Consider not only the end goal (e.g., being a doctor), but the path to that result (pre-med, medical school, residency, fellowship), and make sure that you are able to stomach the sacrifices that it may entail. As Mark Manson asks, "What's your favorite flavor of shit sandwich?"
5. Be careful to ignore *sunk costs* when deciding on a career change. No matter how much money or time you (or your parents) have invested in a certain path, remember that your future should be decided on its own merits, not based on historical baggage.

To summarize,

– Since we have no way of predicting whether we will enjoy a particular job, and
– It is unlikely that we will, in fact, enjoy it,[5]
– We should assume that we are not going to enjoy our job,
– And then be pleasantly surprised if we do.

Now, this is a facile statement—"assume you will hate it and then if you don't that's great"—but it has the benefit of being both accurate and efficacious. Lowering our expectations can work to our advantage here. The alternative approach, which seems to be the default approach of most people, is to continually strive to find a job you love, which is, *statistically speaking*, setting yourself up for a lifetime of disappointment!

POSSESSIONS

The advertising industry has worked hard to convince us that we need certain clothing, automobiles, and electronics. But really, how happy does your phone make you? Would you be miserable if it had a slightly smaller screen or its camera had fewer megapixels? Wouldn't you just get used to it?

More pernicious still is the treadmill of new products on which we are encouraged to climb and run like desperate hamsters. Clothes go out of fashion, cars quickly seem outdated, and televisions become obsolete. And because human instinct is to keep moving forward, once you purchase a product, you are also committing to future purchases of other, newer, more expensive products to satisfy this urge.

Clearly, there are financial reasons why this approach is not optimal. In addition, there are increasingly important considerations around environmental sustainability. For the purposes of this chapter, though, let's focus on developing an attitude towards material possessions that will allow us to maximize our happiness.

The first key is to not spend too much time thinking about which possessions we want to purchase. This is important not only since this time is effectively wasted, but also because there is an inverse relationship between the time spent considering a purchase and the satisfaction with that purchase, as discussed in chapter 6. The "paradox of choice" reminds us that with too many potential options and too much time spent considering these options, we are likely to be disappointed with whatever option we choose. For most small purchases, making a satisficing decision is ideal, but remember to use the SINCERE framework for larger ones.

The second key when considering possessions is to concentrate your anticipated pleasure from your possessions into a few objects. As Marie Kondo recommends, find a small number of objects that "spark joy," and focus on those while purging the rest.[6] Of course, there are many possessions that are simply utilitarian and play an important role in your life—nail clippers and spatulas, for example. Your life is not enriched by these objects, but it sure would be annoying not to have them. However, the goal is to view these objects as means to an end and not spend too much time, money, or emotional investment on their acquisition—again, make satisficing decisions. Enjoy a particularly soft sweater, but don't buy four or spend too much time agonizing over which color suits you best.

The third key is to remember that you will almost certainly lose interest in objects over time. If you can keep this in mind while buying them and envision your future self getting bored with them, then you will attach less importance to the objects. This will also help reduce any feelings of jealousy you may have that others have shinier playthings than you.

Finally, keep in mind the reasons why you buy objects in the first place. Do you really need or even want them? As one financial journalist put it, "We buy things with money we don't have to impress people we don't like."[7] Try to avoid doing too much of that!

HEALTH AND SLEEP

It won't surprise you to hear that leading a healthy lifestyle with regular exercise, reasonable eating habits, and good sleep will benefit not only your longevity but your happiness as well. We already discussed the *mind-body connection* in chapter 2, where your physical vigor influences your mental health and vice versa. However, for many younger people, health is something that is taken for granted, especially if the negative consequences of certain decisions won't be felt for decades. While health itself doesn't lead to happiness, poor health is one of the largest contributors to unhappiness (health is a *necessary* but not *sufficient* condition to being happy). As such, it is important to consider the impact of bad health on our happiness in a prospective "what if" manner, as described later in this chapter. For example, what if you couldn't walk a mile without assistance, how would that impact your happiness? It would probably detract from it quite a bit.

Deep breathing and *meditation* are activities that are deservedly getting more attention and practitioners, aided by easy-to-use apps that allow flexibility in their practice. While meditation may not appeal to everyone as a regular practice, it is well worth considering as a way of calming your body and mind. High levels of stress and the accompanying hormones can damage your body and lead to a variety of physical and mental ailments. Deep breathing and meditation help to reduce stress, as deep breathing sends the physiological message to your brain of "calm down, there is no imminent danger." As such, everyone should give meditation a try, and while many will not stick with it, deep breathing is something that we all can and should do on a regular basis. (Why don't you take a few deep breaths right now? No, really, you should. I'll wait.)

It is perhaps obvious that getting enough *sleep* makes you a more physically and mentally fit person, allows you to be alert during the day, and helps you make better decisions. You may be surprised to hear, though, that chronic sleep deprivation can shorten your lifespan.[8] That's correct: sleeping under five hours per night can lead to a 15 percent higher mortality risk![9] The mechanism for this is somewhat unclear, though it seems reasonable that if sleep is our brain's way of repairing damage that was done during the waking hours, a chronic deficit of this repair time may take an eventual toll.

Finally, you should remember that humans are animals, and thus have a strong and important connection to the natural world. This includes *exercise* and general fitness, which keeps you in good physical and emotional health, but sometimes require some *activation energy* to get you off the couch (having an exercise partner is a good way to get over this hump). More generally, activities in the *outdoors*—hiking, walking, or swimming—remind us of this connection and nourish our soul.[10] There's nothing sadder than a malnourished soul!

EXPLICIT GRATITUDE

We have discussed (in *marginal costs* in chapter 4) how the mind acclimates to its environment by habituation, requiring greater stimulus to produce an equivalent reaction. Similar ground was covered in our discussion of *expectations* and the fact that it is relative, not absolute results that generally please or upset us. Unfortunately, the human brain works the same way with happiness—that which makes us happy will soon be taken for granted, as our brain forces us to run faster on our self-imposed hedonic treadmill.[11] Fortunately (and a bit bizarrely), it is not too difficult to trick our brain into working in reverse, reminding ourselves of how lucky we are and how happy we should be as a result.

The methodology for this is owed to the Stoics, Greek philosophers whose writings date from roughly 300 BCE. One of their goals was to increase their own happiness through mental exercises such as meditation, practicing mental tranquility, and negative visualization. It is on this last approach that we will focus here.

Negative visualization involves the highly macabre process of imagining some gnarly worst-case scenarios (your family lying dead, your body wracked by a serious disease, living in a post-apocalyptic world) and then reminding yourself that, in fact, these are not your realities. In other words, you are forcing your mind to reset its gratitude for all the good fortune that you enjoy, appreciating it anew. Admittedly, it feels kind of strange to do this, but if you try it, you might be surprised to find that it works.

A slightly less aggressive form of this is to practice gratitude by making a list each day of that for which you are thankful. Keeping a "gratitude journal" is helpful in this endeavor, and there are many pre-printed options available from your favorite online retailer, as well as apps for your favorite phone. Even taking simple steps such as chewing your food more slowly to savor it or making random positive comments to friends (or strangers) can improve your mental state and your overall happiness.

Another practice of the Stoics was to appreciate that much of life is not in one's control. Life takes many turns, and sometimes "shit happens"; as such, it is best not to incur unnecessary stress or worry about staying on a particular path. There is a children's book titled *Zen Shorts*[12] that contains some stylized versions of Zen koans (riddles designed to enlighten their readers), and it was my children's favorite read-aloud book when they were younger.[13] One of these tells the story of a farmer whose life takes a series of positive and negative turns, after each of which his neighbors exclaim, "What good luck!" or "What bad luck!" The farmer, with unflappable equanimity, replies each time, "Maybe." And it turns out that what appears to be good news is in fact bad, and vice versa.

Life is a journey, and it is not immediately obvious which developments are beneficial and which are harmful at the time. Easy and unearned success may set you up for a lifetime of future disappointment, as many lottery winners realize.[14] Meanwhile, a temporary setback (see "The Value of Failure" in chapter 7, for example) may reveal a whole new opportunity or path of advancement—it could be the best thing that ever happened to you!

This is another reason why it is crucial to remember and apply the concept of *perspective*. How you view something may be as important as the thing itself. Attempt to see the proverbial glass as half full whenever possible. And remember not to attach too much importance to any given event, as it will surely fade with the fullness of time.

SOCIAL CONNECTIONS

Humans are social creatures who derive energy and satisfaction from belonging to a larger community. These connections, which come from interactions with friends, family, coworkers, interest groups, or volunteering activities, remind us that we are integral parts of a greater whole. It is important to foster these connections and appreciate the relationships we have. Valuing your friendships, and working to maintain and nurture them, is vital to leading a happy and fulfilled life.

Looking back at the *hierarchy of needs*, we see "love and belonging" in the middle of the pyramid. In other words, this sense of belonging is central to a foundation of emotional health, coming just after a sense of safety. Having this support will also allow you to tackle some of the self-actualization goals higher up the pyramid.

Conversely, there are aspects of social interactions that can lead to unhappiness and should be avoided. The evolutionary purpose of envy may have been to motivate an individual to gather social status to further her power and genetic line. In the animal kingdom, male elephant seals aim to occupy the top of the social pyramid (becoming the "beachmaster"), and all the lesser bull seals use their envy of the beachmaster to drive them to grow stronger. Since the "beachmaster" is the only male that gets to mate with the harem of up to one hundred females, there is a lot of envy and probably plenty of unhappiness!

A related concept is FOMO, which is rooted in the anxiety we feel about being part of a group whose shared experiences are being formed without us. Not being part of that collective memory could (in theory) distance us from the group, which would have implications for our own status and survival. In today's world, it is much more likely that your feelings are overblown compared to the actual social benefit or damage that might result. Our fast-thinking brains have put too much importance on these considerations, and we must consciously downplay these impulses to restore the balance.

COMPARATIVE ADVANTAGE AND TIME

Time is precious, and as a result we must frequently forgo desirable activities. There used to be a saying: "Family, friends, career, exercise, and sleep—choose three of these, since you can't have all five."[15] A work-life balance is struck differently for everyone, though these trade-offs can be minimized when recalling that it is not truly a *zero-sum game*. For example, the advent of hybrid work schedules has allowed the recapture of significant commuting hours and increased flexibility to stay home for childcare or medical needs.

We can also use our time more efficiently and effectively, freeing it up for other pursuits. One way to do this is to apply the model of *comparative advantage*. Outsourcing certain basic activities such as cleaning, cooking, dog-walking, and laundry can free up valuable time for other activities. While it seems self-indulgent to do this, there may be a reasonable economic basis for it. If a laundry service can use a large washer and an assembly-line approach to do a load of laundry more quickly and cheaply than you can, then why not take advantage of that arbitrage? The *opportunity cost* of cooking a meal can easily be higher than the cost of takeout food if the preparation absorbs an hour of your valuable time. So, within reason (and budget), maximize the time spent on productive and enjoyable activities by outsourcing certain time sinks.

Within this context, it is also instructive to consider the various *bottlenecks* present in your life. In what areas or activities are your resources constrained? Are there small changes that can be made which will lead to significant overall improvement? For example, are you a very slow typist, which leads to spending an inordinate amount of time preparing reports? Consider taking a speed-typing course online or using dictation software. Are you unable to choose an outfit in the morning, making you late to work? Perhaps you should narrow down your wardrobe to just a few options, like the Zuck.

MENTAL WELLNESS

Anxiety, depression, and other disorders seem to be more common in our modern world, or at least more frequently diagnosed and addressed. An effective tool for helping with many of these disorders is cognitive behavioral therapy, or CBT. This therapy teaches people to reframe their negative thoughts and then employ various techniques to counteract them. In effect, people are taking control of their minds and applying a rational lens to patterns of self-destructive behavior. This is the essence of an effective mental model!

Many of the negative feelings that permeate our lives are irrational or blown out of proportion. Having tools that allow us to contextualize, explain, and ameliorate a difficult situation, or get ourselves out of a cycle of negativity, can be extremely useful. While I will not delve into the deeper theory or mechanics of CBT here, and I urge you to seek professional assistance if you feel that it might be of use, there are several websites listed at the end of this book that will give you an introduction to this therapeutic practice.

I have known many people who were helped by CBT methods, and I think it is well worth consideration. More generally, the success of this therapy for millions of people with a wide range of disorders should remind us that our mind is both flawed and malleable and give us all confidence that we can improve its functioning with a modicum of effort.

TEMPORAL HAPPINESS

"Happiness" is a broad term, and it is unhelpful to consider it as a monolithic construct. Specifically, there are many decisions we make that cause us to be happy in the short term (hours, days, weeks) but unhappy in the long term (months, years, decades), and vice versa. You could decide to blow off a work deadline and spend the evening out with friends, which would increase your happiness that night. But there might be a host of negative consequences, especially if you did this too frequently, which would likely lead to lower levels of happiness in the future. As an extreme example, trying heroin will likely feel pretty good for a few hours, but will negatively impact your happiness for the rest of your life.

Just like with *discounted cash flows*, we need to accept a tradeoff between happiness today and happiness tomorrow. In general, we should be willing to sacrifice some happiness today to enjoy more of it tomorrow—called "delayed gratification." Whenever we stay home to study for a test instead of going to a friend's party, we defer gratification to increase our future happiness. However, finding this balance is an individual process. While we don't want to ignore the future, we also don't want to live for the future at the expense of the present.

A related concept is what psychologists call the "peak-end rule." Human brains, when forming memories of an experience, tend to only capture the extremes and the final mental snapshot—not the complete set of feelings. Otherwise, we would be overwhelmed by all the information contained in our memories, which is not particularly useful for survival. So, if you think back to your last vacation, you will not remember every day of it, but rather the highlights, the lowlights, and how you felt at its end (energized, relaxed, disappointed, or tired).[16] On a smaller scale, when you are eating a piece of chocolate cake, you will only remember the final bite, not the dozen bites before it. So, it's probably not worth taking more than a few bites, as you won't remember most of them, but you will retain the calories! In general, if you are attempting to maximize the happiness you feel when recollecting an experience, you will take different actions than if you are trying to enjoy the moment.[17]

DRUGS, SMOKING, AND ALCOHOL

Public service announcement (that you already know): drugs and alcohol not only won't make you happy but have the potential to make you profoundly unhappy. In moderation, each can facilitate social interactions, which is a positive outcome, but both can also lead to very negative social interactions, some of which can be life-altering. Even worse, drugs and alcohol in excess can derail your life and those of the people around you. The addictive nature of these substances makes consuming too much of them a very common outcome.

The Grant Study was a psychological study begun in 1938 on 268 Harvard students.[18] They were all male, but their backgrounds were varied, and their careers ran the gamut from President of the United States (John F. Kennedy) to a variety of (mostly white-collar) middle class professions. This study is still ongoing and currently has over eighty years of data about what leads to a happy and fulfilled life. The main conclusions were as follows:

1. Strong relationships are incredibly important (see the earlier section on *social connections*)—as the study director put it, "Happiness is love."
2. Consumption of alcohol and tobacco is the single largest predictor of unhappiness.

Now, going back to our *causation versus correlation* section, let me be the first to admit that alcohol could be the symptom, not the cause, of this unhappiness. In this case, though, it seems to be mostly the cause, based on what the researchers can tell. Additionally, alcohol and tobacco have the dual impact of hurting your happiness indirectly (through their impact on health outcomes) and directly (through the emotional damage they inflict on your relationships). Let's add these to the reasons why they should only be enjoyed in moderation!

PUTTING IT ALL TOGETHER

In summary, to maximize your happiness, you should:

- **Reduce** the time and energy devoted to activities that are unlikely to make you happy (finding the perfect job, accumulating possessions, consuming drugs and alcohol, or performing tedious tasks).
- **Increase** the time and energy devoted to activities that are likely to make you happy (new experiences, social interactions, or rewarding hobbies).
- Maintain an appropriate **context** and perspective by incorporating mindfulness and explicit gratitude into your daily routine.
- Remember the importance of physical **health** (spend more time outdoors) and mental health (employ CBT to overcome emotional roadblocks).

And so, we have another acronym to add to the arsenal:

Reduce the bad.
Increase the good.
Context is key.
Health is better than wealth.

At this point you may as well *pause*, think, and consider whether you are **RICH** in happiness, or whether you could reduce, increase, add context, or improve your health. Going back to the first point made in this framework, *pause to think* about whether your work/life balance is struck appropriately, or if your priorities should be shifted. These are questions that only you can answer, but please, please, please—answer them!

A Fond Farewell

I hope you have enjoyed our whirlwind tour of mental models. As stated in the introduction, my hope is that this book has provided an efficient introduction to the topic and elucidated important concepts and frameworks to help you think more clearly, decide more effectively, and be a happier person.

If you continue with your mental models journey, great! I'm glad to have awakened a sense of intellectual curiosity on the topic and have provided a nice long list of recommended further reading. If you were especially entertained by the comics throughout, full color versions are available at https://pausementalmodels.com/cartoons. If this is the last book on mental models that you will ever read, also great! I'm happy that I covered the bases in such a satisfactory manner that you feel no need to look any further. If you hated the book, let me know—I'll refund my dollar of royalties. But I really hope this wasn't the case.

For your reference, here are the terms and acronyms I mentioned along the way:

Biases	Decisions	Learning	Happiness
Self-esteem	Satisfice	Who?	Reduce the bad
Stories not stats	Information	What?	Increase the good
Snap judgments	Narrow down	Where?	Context is key
	Checklist	When?	Health
	Expectations	Why?	
	Regrets	How?	
	Embrace emotion		

The longer discussions on investing and understanding should also be kept in the back of your mind. Pull them out (either physically or meta-phorically!) when you *pause to think* about a situation more carefully.

Thanks for your attention, and good luck with everything!

Jaime Lester
New York City
2024

Answers to Exercises

THE MIND-BODY CONNECTION

1. This is the mind-body connection!
2. No, pain is a valuable signaling mechanism, and should be understood as such.
3. This is the release of endorphins after long periods of exercise.

UTILITARIANISM

1. Add them all up, and the lowest number is best—bowling = 8, ping pong = 9, movie = 7.
2. Choice a) seems just a little bit wrong, but the others all seem reasonable.
3. Try to get the most nutrition for the money you have—optimize for calories per dollar with a minimum of certain nutrients. Probably lots of beans and pasta!

HIERARCHY OF NEEDS

1. There are lots of reasonable answers here, and a smartphone is one of them!

2. Either it doesn't or they have found a way to shrink their base needs compared to what others require.
3. Many people do feel satisfaction at being highly competent at a certain activity, but the data probably don't support this assertion.

THE GOLDEN RULE

1. "Don't hit (Bobby), since you wouldn't like it if he hit you; don't take (Bobby's) snack, since you wouldn't like it if he took yours."
2. It can be frustrating, as other people can take advantage of you if you follow it and they don't. This is a different formulation of the "free rider" problem. But you should still follow the Golden Rule, even so!
3. Yes for many values (like the sanctity of life), but no for some others (e.g., variations in individual versus group prioritization).

RECIPROCITY

1. Do what you are comfortable doing, but don't feel obliged to give him anything—you didn't ask for the trinket!
2. Say no! One thing has nothing to do with the other—you already paid her back the money.
3. When viewed using the lens of reciprocity, while also remembering that judgment is impaired by alcohol, we can probably agree that this norm should probably be rethought!

OCCAM'S RAZOR

1. No, it is overwhelmingly likely to be pain from overexertion.
2. Computational power costs money and takes time—the less, the better.
3. The last one—and unfortunately for students, teachers aren't dumb!

INVERSION

1. It could ask itself all the ways to design advertising that would alienate its customer, hurt its brand, and disparage its products. Then, it would make sure it was not doing any of those things.

2. Once you are aware of areas that are especially problematic, you can pay special attention to them. Removing potential points of failure will increase the chances of success.

3. It is common to focus on investment returns, but it is easier and likely more profitable to remove unnecessary expenses. These include credit card debt, bank fees (and cash deposits that aren't earning interest), and extraneous household costs.

PERSPECTIVE

1. This simple act reframes perspective to focus on the positive aspects of a situation instead of the negative ones.

2. Expectations tend to determine levels of happiness and satisfaction, which feeds into one's outlook and interpretation of a situation.

3. Understanding the perspective of those who work at various levels within a company can reveal significant positives and negatives about its culture and inner workings.

EXPECTATIONS

1. It could be that a) people expected earnings to decline more than 50 percent, b) Tesla raised expectations for earnings in future periods, or c) some other metric excited investors.

2. This is an example of happiness being shaped by relative expectations versus absolute result.

3. Lowering or "managing" expectations, so that they could be exceeded.

RISK VERSUS REWARD

1. This is expected value again, and the first is the better investment, at $137.50 versus $100.

2. The cost of tuition and the opportunity cost of not working during your time at school.

3. Your friend may have different calculations around the rewards and risks of the investment. Additionally, people have different preferences and attach different implied values to risks and rewards.

COMPOUND INTEREST

1. 1.12^{10}, or \$311.
2. Because if this were true, a young investor could invest \$1,000 into stocks and would have \$500 million when she retired. Think about that for a second!
3. Various concepts can build on each other, so new learning can bring deeper understanding when applied to previously held knowledge.

CHECKLISTS

1. Recipes, grocery/packing lists, and to-do lists.
2. If you can't simplify something, you can always break it into smaller parts.
3. Mnemonics, checklist apps, or a Sharpie marker on your palm.

REDUNDANCY

1. Pack clothing that is multi-use, like zip-off pants and lots of layers.
2. Build it in a location not prone to earthquakes or power outages, but ideally have at least two locations.
3. Because they are likely to experience one at some point and then will have to borrow money to pay it.

FEEDBACK LOOPS

1. If true: shots are made, the shooter has more confidence/energy/mental focus, which leads to more shots being made. If not: shots are made, shooter becomes overconfident, gets sloppy, and misses shots.
2. a) Yes; b) No; c) Yes this is a feedback loop, but it is not beneficial (just ask my overweight dog, Coco!).
3. Each player must juggle one more time than the previous player.

ACTIVATION ENERGY

1. This depends on a lot of factors, including the cost of the chemical catalyst, time sensitivity, etc.
2. You could have a friend pick you up, institute some reward/penalty for yourself, or cancel Netflix.
3. Maybe, though it isn't ideal and it's probably best not to rely on it too heavily.

DECISION VERSUS OUTCOME

1. a) Bad Decision/Good Outcome; b) BD/GO; c) GD/BO; d) BD/BO; e) BD/GO.
2. That this was a bad decision with a good outcome.
3. As a good decision with a bad outcome.

LEVERAGE

1. Everything but the sponge (which is kind of a fun name for a band, right?).
2. The home price doubled ($1 million goes to $2 million), but you made 6× on your equity ($200,000 goes to $1.2 million).
3. Use your trucks to deliver the beverages at the same time.

SUNK COST

1. No—You should give away or sell the tickets, but even if you can't, you should go to the show, not the concert.
2. No—Give it away, wrap it for later, or even throw it out.
3. This depends—If an A is important, switch. Otherwise make the best of it and figure out how to not make the same mistake the next time.

EXPECTED VALUE

1. −$.50, before taxes.
2. $2,500 = $5,000 additional cost ($20,000 of lease payments + $35,000 buyout cost less $50,000 initial purchase price) × 50 percent chance of buying the car.
3. You will save an hour: 3 hours versus 4. You will spend $48 of gas instead of $36, plus the $10 expected cost of the ticket, so $22 expected cost for the hour saved.

INCENTIVES

1. No, he will let the room grow messier in order to get paid to clean it.
2. No, sometimes focusing on incentives just isn't appropriate since this misses the whole point of volunteering!

3. One eighty-hour week followed by one week off to earn more overtime pay for the same hours worked.

DECLINING MARGINAL UTILITY

1. Ice cream has a declining marginal benefit, so you will grow tired of it.
2. People already got the benefits of a larger screen, and the other features are not as important.
3. It takes a fixed amount of time to cook, so he is only charging for the additional (marginal) cost of the pasta.

NEGOTIATIONS

1. There are many. One example is for Juan to trade Mounds to Quinn in exchange for Kit Kats, etc.
2. Your boss could allow you to leave to pick up kids and then return to work, work from home, or work 7 A.M. to 3 P.M. instead of 9 A.M. to 5 P.M.
3. You could charge him up to $50 million since he otherwise has no way to profit from the money he has already spent. This is known in real estate as a "hold up."

COMPARATIVE ADVANTAGE

1. Yes, if you can't find someone else cheaper, since it's still more efficient for you to work instead of spending your time cleaning.
2. For the team, yes, since his greatest comparative advantage is as a goalie. For Toby, maybe, depending on how much he likes playing goalie.
3. To have a comparative advantage versus other college applicants by focusing on less competitive skills and geographies.

GAME THEORY AND DEDUCTIVE REASONING

1. No one will get any money, since it is too difficult to coordinate everyone, and at least one person will try to cheat.
2. You could collude with the other bidder to minimize the bid price and then flip a coin to see who gets the painting.
3. You could remove your steering wheel, demonstrating a "credible commitment" to not swerving.

NETWORK EFFECTS AND ECONOMIES OF SCALE

1. Religions, political parties, sports leagues, and internet standards.
2. An investment fund that gets too large to invest in smaller companies, a business that attracts government regulation due to its size, and large bureaucracies with slow response times.
3. a) Nothing or perhaps a small economy of scale; b) Economy of scale; c) Network effect; d) Nothing.

ADVERSE SELECTION AND MORAL HAZARD

1. So that only healthy people who could climb stairs would enroll and the insurance companies would likely pay less for their medical care.
2. Offer warranties, get customer references, or pay for third-party inspections.
3. No, it probably doesn't work, and it is likely stolen to boot!

BOTTLENECKS

1. Buy another sharpener to match the pencil-making capacity.
2. Comprehension mostly, and some vocabulary.
3. Left-handed lay-ups, duh!

CORRELATION VERSUS CAUSATION

1. Lice don't like higher temperatures and leave the body of someone who has a high fever, so the causality is reversed.
2. Perhaps, but maybe since eyesight is hereditary, perhaps parents with bad eyesight needed the light on to read.
3. No, this is most likely due to the correlation of hotter temperatures and swimming frequency. But certain ice cream (bubblegum-flavored, especially) should be outlawed anyway!

STATISTICAL SIGNIFICANCE

1. There are six colors of M&Ms in roughly equal proportions. So, the chance of drawing five reds from a standard assortment is roughly $\frac{1}{6} \times \frac{1}{6} \times \frac{1}{6} \times \frac{1}{6} \times \frac{1}{6}$, or 1 in 7,800. So, he might be right. Or it might be just red and green

M&Ms (a Christmas mix), in which case all reds would come out ½ × ½ × ½ × ½ × ½, or 1 in 32 times. This is obviously much more likely.

2. The study could be correct, but more data is needed to draw the conclusion, since it could easily just be a random variation.

3. Nothing; the sample size is far too small. Plus, you shouldn't stereotype in the first place!

MEAN REVERSION

1. It is likely to revert to the mean and thus underperform going forward, so don't buy it.

2. Probably nothing, as you will lose them naturally as your body compensates. However, for significant weight loss, you will have to restrict calories (with or without the help of weight-loss drugs).

3. There are lots of high cards coming, which favors the player (the dealer will "bust" more frequently), so you should increase your bet size. This isn't mean reversion, though; it's probability.

Resources and Recommended Reading

Cognitive Biases

Ariely, Dan. *Predictably Irrational*. New York: HarperCollins, 2008.

Berger, Jonah. *Invisible Influence*. New York: Simon & Schuster, 2016.

Bevelin, Peter. *Seeking Wisdom: From Darwin to Munger*. Malmo, Sweden: Post Scriptum, 2007.

Brockman, John, ed. *This Will Make You Smarter*. New York: Harper Perennial, 2012.

"Cognitive Biases Books." Goodreads, accessed April 8, 2023. https://www.goodreads .com/shelf/show/cognitive-biases.

Desjardins, Jeff. "24 Cognitive Biases That are Warping Your Perception of Reality," Visual Capitalist, November 26, 2021. https://www.visualcapitalist.com/24 -cognitive-biases-warping-reality/.

Dobelli, Rolf. *The Art of the Good Life*. New York: Hachette, 2017.

Dobelli, Rolf. *The Art of Thinking Clearly*. New York: Harper, 2014.

Dwyer, Christopher. "12 Common Biases That Affect How We Make Everyday Decisions," *Psychology Today*, September 7, 2018. https://www.psychologytoday .com/us/blog/thoughts-thinking/201809/12-common-biases-affect-how-we -make-everyday-decisions.

Easterly, William. "Michael Lewis's 'Brilliant' New Book About Cognitive Bias," *Wall Street Journal*, December 5, 2016. https://www.wsj.com/articles/michael -lewiss-brilliant-new-book-about-cognitive-bias-1480982097.

Fine, Cordelia. *A Mind of Its Own*. New York: Norton, 2008.

Gilovich, Thomas. *How We Know What Isn't So*. New York: Free Press, 2008.

Harford, Tim. *The Undercover Economist*. New York: Oxford University Press, 2006.

Kahneman, Daniel. *Thinking Fast and Slow*. New York: Farrar, Straus and Giroux, 2011.

Kaufman, Peter, ed. *Poor Charlie's Almanack*. Marcelline, MO: Walsworth, 2005.

Lagnado, David. *Explaining the Evidence*. Cambridge: Cambridge University Press, 2021.

Levitt, Steven, and Stephen Dubner. *Think Like a Freak*. New York: William Morrow, 2014.

McRaney, David. *You Are Now Less Dumb*. New York: Gotham, 2013.

Thaler, Richard. *Misbehaving*. New York: Norton, 2015.
"20 Best Cognitive Biases Books of All Time." Bookauthority, accessed April 8, 2023. https://bookauthority.org/books/best-cognitive-biases-books.
"25 Cognitive Biases," accessed April 8, 2023. http://25cognitivebiases.com/.
Weinberg, Gabriel, and Lauren McCann. *Super Thinking*. New York: Portfolio, 2019.

Expected Value

"Mean (Expected Value) of a Discrete Random Variable." Khan Academy, accessed April 9, 2023. https://www.khanacademy.org/math/ap-statistics/random-variables-ap/discrete-random-variables/v/expected-value-of-a-discrete-random-variable.
Starmer, Josh. "Expected Values, Main Ideas!!!" StatQuest on YouTube, accessed April 9, 2023. https://www.youtube.com/watch?v=KLs_7b7SKi4.

Mind-Body

Haidt, Jonathan. *The Righteous Mind*. New York: Pantheon, 2012.
Keyser, Hannah. "A Brief and Bizarre History of the Baby Cage." Mental Floss, June 24, 2015. http://mentalfloss.com/article/65496/brief-and-bizarre-history-baby-cage.
Reuben, Aaron. "The Incredible Link Between Nature and Your Emotions." Outside, June 11, 2019. https://www.outsideonline.com/2397694/nature-mental-health.
"Sour Mood Getting You Down? Get Back to Nature." Harvard Health Publishing, March 30, 2021. https://www.health.harvard.edu/mind-and-mood/sour-mood-getting-you-down-get-back-to-nature.

Probability

Online courses on productivity are found here:
https://www.coursera.org/learn/introductiontoprobability.
https://www.edx.org/learn/probability.
https://www.khanacademy.org/math/statistics-probability/probability-library.
Ellenberg, Jordan. *How Not to Be Wrong*. London: Penguin, 2014.
Rumsey, Deborah. *Probability for Dummies*. Hoboken, NJ: Wiley, 2006.

DECISION-MAKING

Duke, Annie. *How to Decide*. New York: Portfolio, 2020.
Duke, Annie. *Thinking in Bets*. New York: Portfolio, 2018.
Einhorn, Cheryl Strauss. *Problem Solved*. Wayne, NJ: Career, 2017.
Goldsmith, Marshall. *The Earned Life*. New York: Currency, 2022.

Grant, Adam. *Think Again*. New York: Viking, 2021.

Hardy, Darren. *The Compound Effect*. New York: Hachette, 2010.

Heath, Chip, and Dan Heath. *Decisive*. New York: Currency, 2013.

Koch, Richard. *The 80/20 Principle*. New York: Currency, 1998.

Konnikova, Maria. *The Biggest Bluff*. London: Penguin, 2020.

Mauboussin, Michael. *Think Twice*. Boston: Harvard Business School Publishing, 2009.

Neuwirth, Peter. *What's Your Future Worth?* Oakland, CA: Berrett-Koehler, 2015.

Parrish, Shane. *Clear Thinking*. New York: Portfolio, 2023.

Plous, Scott. *The Psychology of Judgment and Decision Making*. New York: McGraw-Hill, 1993.

LEARNING METHODS

Deliberate Practice

Clear, James. "The Beginner's Guide to Deliberate Practice." Jamesclear.com, accessed April 10, 2023. https://jamesclear.com/beginners-guide-deliberate-practice.

Colvin, Geoff. *Talent Is Overrated*. New York: Portfolio, 2008.

Coyle, Daniel. *The Talent Code*. New York: Bantam, 2009.

Eliason, Nat. "45 Deliberate Practice Examples for Rapidly Improving Your Skills." Nateliason.com, July 3, 2017. https://www.nateliason.com/blog/deliberate-practice-examples.

Ericsson, Anders, and Robert Pool. *Peak*. Boston: Mariner, 2017.

Gladwell, Malcolm. *Outliers*. New York: Little, Brown, 2008.

"How to Master New Skills with Deliberate Practice." BBC Worklife, March 18, 2019. https://www.bbc.com/worklife/article/20190318-how-to-master-new-skills-with-deliberate-practice.

Syed, Matthew. *Bounce*. New York: Harper Perennial, 2011.

Waitzkin, Josh. *The Art of Learning*. New York: Free Press, 2007.

Diffuse versus Focused Thinking

Cleese, John. "Creativity in Management." YouTube, June 21, 2017. https://www.youtube.com/watch?v=Pb5oIIPO62g.

Hunt, Andy. *Pragmatic Thinking & Learning*. Dallas, TX: Pragmatic Bookshelf, 2008.

Newport, Cal. *Deep Work*. New York: Hachette, 2016.

Oakley, Barbara. *A Mind for Numbers*. New York: Penguin, 2014.

Oakley, Barbara, and Terrence Sejnowski. "Introduction to the Focused and Diffuse Modes." Coursera, accessed April 10, 2023. https://www.coursera.org/lecture/learning-how-to-learn/introduction-to-the-focused-and-diffuse-modes-75EsZ.

Memory Techniques

Buzan, Tony. *Mind Map Mastery*. London: Watkins, 2018.

Foer, Jonathan. *Moonwalking with Einstein*. New York: Penguin, 2011.

Gluck, Mark. *Learning and Memory*. New York: Worth, 2019.

Horsley, Kevin. *Unlimited Memory*. TCK, 2016.

Lorayne, Harry. *The Memory Book*. New York: Ballantine, 1974.

"The Memory Techniques Wiki." Accessed April 10, 2023. https://artofmemory .com/wiki/Main_Page.

O'Brien, Dominic. *You Can Have an Amazing Memory*. London: Watkins, 2011.

Schwandt, Jaime. "5 Proven Memorization Techniques to Make the Most of Your Memory." Lifehack, September 28, 2022. https://www.lifehack.org/805775 /memorization-techniques.

Checklists

Gawande, Atul. *The Checklist Manifesto*. New York: Metropolitan, 2009.

Gawande, Atul. "The Checklist." *New Yorker*, December 2, 2007. https://www .newyorker.com/magazine/2007/12/10/the-checklist.

Levitin, Daniel. *The Organized Mind*. New York: Dutton, 2014.

Reading and Note-Taking

Adler, Mortimer, and Charles Van Doren. *How to Read a Book*. New York: Touchstone, 1972.

Ahrens, Sonke. *How to Take Smart Notes*. Hamburg, Germany: Independently Published, 2022.

"Classroom Strategies." UMass Dartmouth, accessed April 10, 2023. https://www .umassd.edu/dss/resources/students/classroom-strategies/.

Ho, Leon. "9 Effective Reading Strategies for Quick Comprehension." LifeHack, February 14, 2023. https://www.lifehack.org/899737/reading-strategies.

"Reading Better: Retaining and Applying What You Read." Farnam Street, accessed April 10, 2023. https://fs.blog/reading/.

"Reading Techniques—Enhance Your Academic Skills." University of the People, accessed April 10, 2023. https://www.uopeople.edu/blog/reading-techniques/.

"SQ3R." Wikipedia, last edited March 28, 2023. https://en.wikipedia.org/wiki/SQ3R.

"The Top 3 Most Effective Ways to Take Notes While Reading." Farnam Street, accessed April 10, 2023. https://fs.blog/taking-notes-while-reading/.

Willingham, Daniel. *Outsmart Your Brain*. New York: Gallery, 2023.

Problem-Solving

Holyoak, Keith J., and Robert G. Morrison, eds. *The Oxford Handbook of Thinking and Reasoning*. New York: Oxford University Press, 2012.

Watanabe, Ken. *Problem Solving 101*. New York: Portfolio, 2009.

Growth Mindset

"Carol Dweck: A Summary of Growth and Fixed Mindsets." Farnam Street, accessed April 10, 2023. https://fs.blog/2015/03/carol-dweck-mindset/.
Duckworth, Angela. *Grit*. New York: Scribner, 2016.
Dweck, Carol. *Mindset*. New York: Random House, 2016.
Dweck, Carol. "What Having a 'Growth Mindset' Actually Means." *Harvard Business Review*, January 13, 2016. https://hbr.org/2016/01/what-having-a-growth -mindset-actually-means.
"Growth Mindset Activities." Khan Academy, accessed April 10, 2023. https://www .khanacademy.org/partner-content/learnstorm-growth-mindset-activities-us.
"Growth Mindset vs Fixed Mindset: An Introduction." TEDEd, accessed April 10, 2023. https://ed.ted.com/featured/qrZmOV7R.
https://www.mindsetworks.com/science/ is a website with various pedagogical tools used to encourage students to adopt a growth mindset.
Ricci, Mary Cay. *Nothing You Can't Do*. New York: Routledge, 2021.
Tough, Paul. *How Children Succeed*. New York: First Mariner, 2013.

Failure

Fattal, Isabel. "The Value of Failing." *Atlantic*, April 25, 2018. https://www.theatlantic .com/education/archive/2018/04/the-value-of-failing/558848/.
Gergen, Christoper, and Gregg Vanourek. "The Value of Failure." *Harvard Business Review*, October 2, 2008. https://hbr.org/2008/10/the-value-of-failure.
Losse, Kate. "The Art of Failing Upward." *New York Times*, March 5, 2016. https:// www.nytimes.com/2016/03/06/opinion/sunday/the-art-of-failing-upward .html.
Maney, Kevin. "In Silicon Valley, Failing Is Succeeding." *Newsweek*, August 31, 2015. https://www.newsweek.com/2015/09/11/silicon-valley-failing-succeeding -367179.html.
Schulz, Kathryn. *Being Wrong*. New York: HarperCollins, 2010.
Syed, Matthew. *Black Box Thinking*. New York: Portfolio, 2015.

UNDERSTANDING

Fake News

Davis, Wynne. "Fake or Real?" NPR, December 5, 2016. https://www.npr.org/sections /alltechconsidered/2016/12/05/503581220/fake-or-real-how-to-self-check-the -news-and-get-the-facts.
"Fake News." BBC, accessed April 10, 2023. https://www.bbc.com/news/topics /cjxv13v27dyt/fake-news.

Kiely, Eugene, and Lori Robertson. "How to Spot Fake News." FactCheck.org, November 18, 2016. https://www.factcheck.org/2016/11/how-to-spot-fake-news/.

Levitin, Daniel. *A Field Guide to Lies*. New York: Dutton, 2019. And a talk by Mr. Levitin is here: https://www.youtube.com/watch?v=3hK7Gd8UgmI.

Paulos, John Allen. *A Mathematician Reads the Newspaper*. New York: Basic, 2013.

Advertising

Cialdini, Robert. *Influence: The Psychology of Persuasion*. New York: Harper Business, 2021.

Eyal, Nir. *Hooked: How to Build Habit-Forming Products*. New York: Portfolio, 2019.

Heath, Robert. "How Ads Manipulate Our Emotions." BBC Ideas, July 30, 2019. https://www.bbc.co.uk/ideas/videos/how-ads-manipulate-our-emotions---and-how-to-resis/p07j581q.

Stroebe, Wolfgang. "How Advertisements Manipulate Behavior." *Scientific American*, May 1, 2012. https://www.scientificamerican.com/article/the-subtle-power-of-hidden-messages/.

Scientific Research

Harford, Tim. *The Data Detective*. New York: Riverhead, 2021.

Pain, Elisabeth. "How to (Seriously) Read a Scientific Paper." *Science*, March 21, 2016. https://www.sciencemag.org/careers/2016/03/how-seriously-read-scientific-paper.

Raff, Jennifer. "How to Read and Understand a Scientific Paper." Huffpost, June 18, 2014. https://www.huffpost.com/entry/how-to-read-and-understand-a-scientific-paper_b_5501628.

Subramanyam, R. V. "Art of Reading a Journal Article: Methodically and Effectively." *Journal of Oral Maxillofacial Pathology* 17, no. 1 (2013): 65–70. https://www.ncbi.nlm.nih.gov/pmc/articles/PMC3687192/.

Zimmer, Carl. "How You Should Read Coronavirus Studies, or Any Science Paper." *New York Times*, June 1, 2020. https://www.nytimes.com/article/how-to-read-a-science-study-coronavirus.html.

INVESTING

www.investforfree.org.

Hagstrom, Robert. *Investing: The Last Liberal Art*. New York: Texere, 2002.

Housel, Morgan. *The Psychology of Money*. Hampshire, UK: Harriman House, 2020.

Pompian, Michael. *Behavioral Finance and Your Portfolio*. Hoboken, NJ: Wiley, 2021.

HAPPINESS

Work

Clifton, John. *Blind Spot*. New York: Simon & Schuster, 2022.

Manson, Mark. *The Subtle Art of Not Giving a F*ck*. New York: HarperOne, 2016.

Rao, Srikumar. *Happiness at Work*. New York: McGraw Hill, 2010.

Simon-Thomas, Emiliana, and Dacher Keltner. "The Foundations of Happiness at Work." BerkeleyX, accessed April 9, 2023. https://www.edx.org/course/the -foundations-of-happiness-at-work.

Spicer, Andre, and Carl Cederstrom. "The Research We've Ignored About Happiness at Work." *Harvard Business Review*, July 21, 2015. https://hbr.org/2015/07 /the-research-weve-ignored-about-happiness-at-work.

Possessions

Becker, Joshua. *The More of Less*. Colorado Springs, CO: WaterBrook, 2016.

Becker, Joshua. "What Is Minimalism?" Becoming Minimalist, November 13, 2019. https://www.becomingminimalist.com/what-is-minimalism/.

Jansson-Boyd, Cathrine. "Can Money Buy You Happiness? It's Complicated." Conversation, October 11, 2016. https://theconversation.com/can-money-buy-you -happiness-its-complicated-66307.

Kondo, Marie. *The Life-Changing Magic of Tidying Up*. San Francisco: Ten Speed, 2014.

Marchal, Jenny. "5 Reasons Why Experiences Make You Happier Than Possessions." LifeHack, April 4, 2018. https://www.lifehack.org/382287/5-reasons-why-experiences -make-you-happier-than-possessions.

Milburn, Josh, and Ryan Nicodemus. *Minimalism*. Missoula, MT: Asymmetrical, 2011.

Pozin, Ilia. "The Secret to Happiness?" *Forbes*, March 3, 2016. https://www.forbes .com/sites/ilyapozin/2016/03/03/the-secret-to-happiness-spend-money-on -experiences-not-things/#77f2084439a6.

Stoicism

Fraenkel, Carlos. "Can Stoicism Make Us Happy?" *Nation*, February 5, 2019. https://www.thenation.com/article/archive/massimo-pigliucci-modern-stoicism -book-review/.

Holiday, Ryan. *The Obstacle Is the Way*. New York: Portfolio, 2014.

Irvine, William. *A Guide to the Good Life*. New York: Oxford University Press, 2009.

Robertson, Donald. *Stoicism and the Art of Happiness*. London: Teach Yourself, 2018.

Sellars, John. "The Secret to Happiness Is Simple: Live Like a Stoic for a Week." *Independent*, September 28, 2018. https://www.independent.co.uk/voices/secret -to-happiness-stoic-epictetus-wellness-a8559126.html.

Shammas, Michael. "Want Happiness? Become a Practicing Stoic." *Huffpost*, January 23, 2014. https://www.huffpost.com/entry/want-happiness-become-a-p_b_3759317.

Mental Wellness/Cognitive Behavioral Therapy

Bettino, Kate. "All About Cognitive Behavioral Therapy." *PsychCentral*, June 2, 2021. https://psychcentral.com/lib/in-depth-cognitive-behavioral-therapy/.

Mcleod, Saul. "Cognitive Behavioral Therapy: Types, Techniques, Uses." *Simply Psychology*, February 8, 2023. https://www.simplypsychology.org/cognitive -therapy.html.

"What Is Cognitive Behavioral Therapy?" American Psychiatric Association, accessed April 9, 2023. https://www.apa.org/ptsd-guideline/patients-and-families/cognitive -behavioral.

Overall Happiness

Dolan, Paul. *Happiness by Design*. New York: Hudson Street, 2014.

Gilbert, Daniel. *Stumbling on Happiness*. New York: Knopf, 2006.

Haidt, Jonathan. *The Happiness Hypothesis*. New York: Basic, 2006.

Harris, Dan. *10 Percent Happier*. New York: HarperCollins, 2014.

Lambert, Craig. "The Talent for Aging Well." *Harvard Magazine*, August 9, 2019. https://harvardmagazine.com/2019/08/the-talent-for-aging-well.

Mineo, Liz. "Good Genes Are Nice, But Joy Is Better." *Harvard Gazette*, April 11, 2017. https://news.harvard.edu/gazette/story/2017/04/over-nearly-80-years-harvard -study-has-been-showing-how-to-live-a-healthy-and-happy-life/.

Pasricha, Neil. *The Happiness Equation*. New York: G. P. Putnam's, 2016.

Rubin, Gretchen. *The Happiness Project*. New York: HarperCollins, 2009.

Santos, Laurie. "The Science of Well-Being." *Coursera*, accessed April 9, 2023. https://www.coursera.org/learn/the-science-of-well-being.

Schwartz, Barry. *The Paradox of Choice*. New York: ECCO, 2016.

Sternbergh, Adam. "Read This Story and Get Happier." *Cut*, May 2005. https:// www.thecut.com/2018/05/how-to-be-happy.html.

Acknowledgments

I would like to thank the following people for their help, support, and inspiration:

Zoë, who was my first and best collaborator on this project, though she may never appreciate how important was her editing.

Quinn, whose independent thinking began long before he could walk, which served as real inspiration for this project.

Cathleen, whose unwavering support has meant the world to me, in this endeavor and throughout our lives together.

Dad, whose love of teaching is infectious—hopefully I was able to channel a fraction of his passion and skill into this book.

Mom, who never met a status quo that she didn't want to challenge and has unapologetically passed that gene on to her children.

Ian, the intellectual Yang to my Yin, who reminds me that it is possible to be too rational at times.

Gisela, one of my oldest friends, who has kept me on my intellectual toes for three decades and counting.

Everyone who has offered suggestions to improve this book, including Jason McDougall, Alix Pasquet, Erik Hartog, Levi Merczel, Sonal Khot, Eli Lifton, Annie Duke, Neeti Madan, Shikhar Ranjan, Monica Lengyel Karlson, David and Hillary Silver, Albert Chen, Tony Sandoval, and, of course, Zoë.

Albertus Ang Hartono, aka Everwinter, for his incredible drawing skills and sunny disposition.

James Wood, for his expert help with the cover design as well as his other artistic contributions to projects through the years.

And to my editors at Columbia University Press: Brian Smith, who guided me through the process with a kind and steady hand, and Myles Thompson, who believed in this project from the start.

Thank you, all.

Jaime Lester
January 2024

Notes

1. COGNITIVE BIASES

1. This analogy comes from Daniel Levitin, *The Organized Mind* (New York: Dutton, 2014), xix, while the "fast" versus "slow" model comes from Daniel Kahneman, *Thinking Fast and Slow* (New York: Farrar, Straus and Giroux, 2011), 20.
2. I'm actually a well-above-average driver, though this is offset by my brother being well-below-average.
3. Including various illusions and puzzles online such as https://www.youtube.com/watch?v=LcpliVYfEqk or https://www.youtube.com/watch?v=rqvadvWZCgU.
4. "List of Cognitive Biases," Wikipedia, last edited April 3, 2023, https://en.wikipedia.org/wiki/List_of_cognitive_biases.
5. Though, given the "replication crisis" discussed in chapter 8, "Understanding," we should be wary of blindly relying on these studies as well.

2. THE HUMANITIES

1. Sai Sun, Ziqing Yao, Jaixin Wei, and Rongjun Yu, "Calm and Smart? A Selective Review of Meditation Effects on Decision Making," *Frontiers in Psychology* 6 (2015): 1059, https://www.ncbi.nlm.nih.gov/pmc/articles/PMC4513203/.
2. Brian Resnick, "The Weird Power of the Placebo Effect, Explained," *Vox*, July 7, 2017, https://www.vox.com/science-and-health/2017/7/7/15792188/placebo-effect-explained.
3. As discussed in Shawn Achor, *The Happiness Advantage* (New York: Crown Business, 2010).
4. A dictionary definition: *Immoral* describes people who can differentiate between right and wrong but intentionally do wrong anyway. *Amoral* implies acknowledgment of what is right and what is wrong but lack of concern for morality when carrying out an act.
5. More about inversion on page 26, and throughout the book.
6. But, seriously, life is not fair.
7. If the tracks are in snow, however, it might be a yeti, since bears hibernate.
8. I still have a long way to go!

9. *The New Yorker*, March 29, 1976, https://www.newyorker.com/magazine/1976 /03/29.
10. As discussed in Gary Bishop, *Unfu*k Yourself* (New York: HarperOne, 2017).
11. Michael Mauboussin, "The Base Rate Book," Credit Suisse, September 26, 2016, https://plus.credit-suisse.com/rpc4/ravDocView?docid=glamqy.

3. INVESTING AND SCIENCE

1. James Montier, "Seven Sins of Fund Management," Dresdner Kleinwort Wasserstein, November 18, 2005, https://www.trendfollowing.com/whitepaper/Seven _Sins_o-DrKW-100436-N.pdf.
2. "Keeping up with the Joneses" is a common statement that reflects this, based on a comic strip from one hundred years ago about a family striving to catch up to their neighbors' material wealth.
3. In fact, winners of bronze medals report themselves to be happier than those who win silver, as they are happy to win any medal at all, while silver medalists are frustrated by how close they came to winning gold.
4. Venture capital, for example, where investors bet on startups with the hopes of discovering the next Amazon, knowing that nine of ten investments will likely fail.
5. Former Secretary of Defense Donald Rumsfeld is most famous for using this framework and titled his memoir *Knowns and Unknowns.*
6. Alex Pasternack, "The Strangest, Most Spectacular Bridge Collapse (and How We Got It Wrong)," *Vice*, December 14, 2015, https://www.vice.com/en/article /kb78w3/the-myth-of-galloping-gertie.
7. Unless they have a banana allergy.
8. "Enzymes Allow Activation Energies to Be Lowered," accessed on April 8, 2023, https://www.nature.com/scitable/content/enzymes-allow-activation -energies-to-be-lowered-14747799/.
9. James Clear, "The Chemistry of Building Better Habits," accessed on April 8, 2023, https://jamesclear.com/chemistry-habits.
10. For instance, say you buy a $100,000 home with a $10,000 down payment (called equity) and a $90,000 mortgage. If the price of the home increases to $110,000, your equity is now worth $20,000 ($110,000 – $90,000 mortgage), which is twice what you invested.
11. Public domain image via OpenClipart-Vectors on https://pixabay.com/vectors /archimedes-lever-quarryman-worker-148273/.
12. Archimedes said that with a long enough lever and a place to stand, he could move the earth, which is technically true but difficult to test in practice!

4. ECONOMICS AND BUSINESS

1. Have you ever studied econometrics? No? Lucky you!
2. Thanks, Mom!

3. Interestingly, this phrase began as a marketing campaign for Pepsi but was quickly adopted in military parlance.
4. In business school lingo, "BATNA," or Best Alternative to Negotiated Agreement.
5. David Ricardo is the main historical proponent of this concept with his 1817 book *On the Principles of Political Economy and Taxation.*
6. The men are told that the hats were selected from a basket that contained two white and three black hats. The men are not allowed to speak unless it is to guess the color of their own hat. If the man who speaks guesses correctly, they are all set free, but if he is incorrect, they will all be sent back to prison for life. Of course, one of the men could simply guess, but if each assumes that the others will behave perfectly logically, a certain answer can be deduced.

    Specifically, if the man standing at the back can see two white hats, he knows his hat is black and will say so (since there are only two white hats in the basket, and he can see both). If he doesn't speak, then he must be seeing either two black hats, or a black and white hat. So, the man in the middle can then deduce that if he sees a white hat, his own hat must be black, and can go ahead and say so. However, if he sees a black hat, he can't know his own hat color, and so will stay silent. Therefore, if both men behind him stay silent, the first man knows that HE must be the one wearing a black hat, can say so, and will free them all.
7. Back in the 1960s, Russia decided to install nuclear missile launchers in Cuba, just a few miles off the coast of Florida. These missiles were a real threat to the security of the U.S. and had to be dealt with before the construction was completed.
8. "Badminton Women's Doubles—Korea v China | London 2012 Olympics," https://www.youtube.com/watch?v=7mq1ioqiWEo&app=desktop; and Jason Hartline, "Badminton and the Science of Rule Making," Huffpost, August 13, 2012, https://www.huffpost.com/entry/badminton-and-the-science-of-rule-making_b_1773988.
9. Let's just ignore the last few decade's (or more) performances of the Mets, Yankees, Rangers, Islanders, Knicks, Nets, Giants, and Jets.
10. "Myspace," Wikipedia, last edited March 26, 2023, https://en.wikipedia.org/wiki/Myspace.
11. Moreso before the Affordable Care Act was passed.
12. Actually, all-you-can-eat sushi might always be a bad idea, regardless of your appetite, since the lower quality of fish that is necessary to make the deal profitable for the restaurant frequently leads to food poisoning.
13. If a car costs $30,000 and lasts 100,000 miles, then the cost per mile driven (of just the car, and ignoring repairs, insurance, gasoline) is $.30. Driving 3,000 miles means the cost of the car (referred to as "depreciation") is $900. So, renting a car for $50 a day makes a lot of sense!
14. From Eliyahu Goldratt, *The Goal* (Great Barrington, MA: North River, 2014).

5. PROBABILITY AND STATISTICS

1. Tyler Vigen, *Spurious Correlations* (New York: Hachette, 2015) and http://www.tylervigen.com/spurious-correlations.
2. Carl Bergstrom and Jevin West, "Criminal Machine Learning," CallingBullshit.org, accessed April 8, 2023, https://callingbullshit.org/case_studies/case_study_criminal_machine_learning.html.
3. For a "normal" distribution, see figure 5.3.
4. This is an example of Bayes' theorem, which we won't get into here, but which you may see in other books on mental models. The theorem deals with probabilities of events that are conditional on information that is already known and is frequently applied to the base rate fallacy and false negatives, as discussed.
5. "Marxism," Wikipedia, last edited April 6, 2023, https://en.wikipedia.org/wiki/Marxism.
6. "Understanding Rabies," The Humane Society of the United States, accessed April 8, 2023, https://www.humanesociety.org/resources/understanding-rabies.
7. "Frederick W. Smith," Wikipedia, last edited March 25, 2023, https://en.wikipedia.org/wiki/Frederick_W._Smith.

6. DECISIONS

1. Malcolm Gladwell, *Talking to Strangers* (New York: Little, Brown, 2019).
2. Iris Bohnet, "How to Take the Bias Out of Interviews," *Harvard Business Review*, April 18, 2016, https://hbr.org/2016/04/how-to-take-the-bias-out-of-interviews.
3. Anthony Tommasini, "To Make Orchestras More Diverse, End Blind Auditions," *New York Times*, July 16, 2020, https://www.nytimes.com/2020/07/16/arts/music/blind-auditions-orchestras-race.html.
4. Michael Schwantes, "The Job Interview Will Soon Be Dead," Inc., accessed April 8, 2023, https://www.inc.com/marcel-schwantes/science-81-percent-of-people-lie-in-job-interviews-heres-what-top-companies-are-.html.
5. Not to be confused with falabellabilities, which are the talents of miniature horses. Please see https://petkeen.com/falabella-horse/. Aren't they cute?
6. This and other algorithms can be found in Brian Christian and Tom Griffiths, *Algorithms to Live By* (New York: Henry Holt, 2016). They also make the reasonable suggestion of prioritizing tasks based on importance per unit of expected time to complete the task.
7. Annie Duke, *How to Decide* (New York: Portfolio, 2020), which is well worth reading.
8. As they used to say in kindergarten.

7. LEARNING

1. Though few of these techniques seem to be particularly helpful, according to this paper: John Dunlosky, Katherine A. Rawson, Elizabeth J. Marsh, Mitchell J.

Nathan, and Daniel T. Willingham, "Improving Students' Learning with Effective Learning Techniques: Promising Directions from Cognitive and Educational Psychology," *Association for Psychological Science*, January 7, 2013, https://www.psychologicalscience.org/publications/journals/pspi/learning-techniques.html.

2. Reading a book cover to cover for pleasure, though, is one on life's greatest delights!
3. There seems to be an opportunity to develop a theory of nine approaches to problem-solving!
4. As popularized by Carol Dweck, *Mindset* (New York: Ballantine, 2008).
5. Nina Semczuk, "A Simple Way to Solve Problems While You Sleep," *muse*, June 19, 2020, https://www.themuse.com/advice/a-simple-way-to-solve-problems-while-you-sleep.
6. For me, at least.
7. Guy Claxton, *Hare Brain, Tortoise Mind* (New York: Ecco, 2004).
8. Such as in Josh Waitzkin, *The Art of Learning* (New York: Free Press, 2007) and Josh Kaufman, *The First 20 Hours* (New York: Portfolio, 2014). Waitzkin is also a big fan of deliberate practice.
9. Here are some examples of this technique: "10 Really Cool Mind Mapping Examples," *MindMaps Unleashed*, accessed April 8, 2023, https://mindmaps unleashed.com/10-really-cool-mind-mapping-examples-you-will-learn-from.
10. I. A. Walker, S. Reshamwalla, and I. H. Wilson, "Surgical Safety Checklists: Do They Improve Outcomes," *BJA: British Journal of Anaesthesia* 109, no. 1 (July 2012): 47–54, https://academic.oup.com/bja/article/109/1/47/237109.
11. Jason Zweig, "A Checklist for Investors," *Wall Street Journal*, December 13, 2013, https://www.wsj.com/articles/SB1000142405270230420220457925479 3231267408.
12. Or at least one of Apple's advertising agencies.
13. As always, it is best to follow Homer Simpson's advice: "The lesson is, never try," https://www.youtube.com/watch?v=NwVNuyfhF0Q.
14. Well, they did before budget cutbacks in 2023 at least!

8. UNDERSTANDING

1. Colgate got in some trouble for this campaign: "Kick in the Teeth over Toothpaste Ads," *Manchester Evening News*, February 15, 2007, https://www .manchestereveningnews.co.uk/news/greater-manchester-news/kick-in-the-teeth-over-toothpaste-ads-979028.
2. https://www.youtube.com/watch?v=xeFoLdeqG1I.
3. Nathaniel Cope and James Spedding, "5 Ways Statistics are Used to Lie to You Every Day," *Cracked*, March 19, 2023, https://www.cracked.com/article _20318_the-5-most-popular-ways-statistics-are-used-to-lie-to-you.html.
4. "Ad Agency to Pay $2 Million for Role in Deceptive Weight Loss and 'Free' Offers," FTC Press Release, February 7, 2018, https://www.ftc.gov/business

-guidance/blog/2018/02/ad-agency-pay-2-million-role-deceptive-weight-loss
-and-free-offers.

5. Brian Ross, Matthew Mosk, Rym Momtaz, and William Gallego, "Caught on Video: Can Herbalife Cure a Brain Tumor?," *ABC News*, April 23, 2014, https://abcnews.go.com/Blotter/caught-tape-herbalife-cures-brain-tumor /story?id=23441488.

6. "ExtenZe," Wikipedia, last edited April 7, 2023, https://en.m.wikipedia.org /wiki/ExtenZe.

7. Andre Smirnov, "Wait! Did an AWD Tesla Cybertruck Pull a 2WD Ford F-150? Behind the Scenes Video," TFL Truck, November 25, 2019, https://www.tfltruck .com/2019/11/wait-did-an-awd-tesla-cybertruck-pull-a-2wd-ford-f-150-behind -the-scenes-video/.

8. Jenny Chang, "The Art of Deceptive Advertising," *Finances Online*, March 6, 2023, https://reviews.financesonline.com/the-art-of-deceptive-advertising -reviewed/.

9. Cara Rosenbloom, "Is This the Secret to Getting Teens to Reject Junk Food?," *Washington Post*, January 1, 2020, https://www.washingtonpost.com/lifestyle /wellness/is-this-the-secret-to-getting-teens-to-reject-junk-food/2019/12/30 /1ed6b096-2378-11ea-a153-dce4b94e4249_story.html.

10. Thomas Gilovich, *How We Know What Isn't So* (New York: Free Press, 2008).

11. If you google any of these topics, you should use the incognito mode on your browser, or you might be served a healthy serving of conspiracy theory ads!

12. James Vincent, "Listen to This AI Voice Clone of Bill Gates Created by Facebook's Engineers," *Verge*, June 10, 2019, https://www.theverge.com/2019 /6/10/18659897/ai-voice-clone-bill-gates-facebook-melnet-speech-generation; James Vincent, "Watch Jordan Peele Use AI to Make Barack Obama Deliver a PSA About Fake News," *Verge*, April 17, 2018, https://www.theverge.com /tldr/2018/4/17/17247334/ai-fake-news-video-barack-obama-jordan-peele -buzzfeed; Tiffany Hsu and Steven Lee Myers, "Can We No Longer Believe Any-thing We See?," *New York Times*, April 8, 2023, https://www.nytimes.com/2023 /04/08/business/media/ai-generated-images.html.

13. Olga Yurkova, "Six Fake News Techniques and Simple Tools to Vet Them," *Global Investigative Journalism Network*, accessed April 8, 2023, https://gijn .org/six-fake-news-techniques-and-simple-tools-to-vet-them/.

14. James Caunt, "People Are Posting Examples of How Media Can Manipulate the Truth," *boredpanda*, accessed April 8, 2023, https://www.boredpanda.com /examples-media-truth-manipulation/?utm_source=google&utm_medium =organic&utm_campaign=organic.

15. John F. Sargent Jr., "The U.S. Science and Engineering Workforce," Congressio-nal Research Service, November 2, 2017, https://fas.org/sgp/crs/misc/R43061 .pdf; "How Many Scientists Exist Worldwide?," Quora, accessed April 8, 2023, https://www.quora.com/How-many-scientists-exist-worldwide.

16. "Nutritionist Loses 27 Pounds on Twinkie and Oreo Diet," *Health Care Business Tech*, November 5, 2010, http://www.healthcarebusinesstech.com/nutritionist -loses-27-pounds-on-twinkie-and-oreo-diet-no-really/.
17. Rosemary Girard, "In 'Live from the Poundstone Institute,' Paula Poundstone is on a Quest for Knowledge," *NPR Extra*, July 6, 2017, https://www.npr.org /sections/npr-extra/2017/07/06/535644657/in-live-from-the-poundstone -institute-paula-poundstone-is-on-a-quest-for-knowled.
18. http://www.snopes.com.
19. "Replication Crisis," Wikipedia, last edited April 1, 2023, https://en.wikipedia .org/wiki/Replication_crisis#Overall; Kelsey Piper, "Science Has Been in a 'Replication Crisis' for a Decade. Have We Learned Anything?," *Vox*, October 14, 2020, https://www.vox.com/future-perfect/21504366/science-replication-crisis -peer-review-statistics.
20. Elisabeth Blik, "Science Has a Nasty Photoshopping Problem," *New York Times*, October 29, 2022, https://www.nytimes.com/interactive/2022/10/29/opinion /science-fraud-image-manipulation-photoshop.html?searchResultPosition=5.
21. Google Scholar provides a metric, ranking publications based on the "h-5 index," which tracks how many times their articles are cited in other papers: https://scholar.google.com/citations?view_op=top_venues.
22. Dawn Chen, "When Correlation Does Not Imply Causation," *Science in the News*, January 27, 2021, https://sitn.hms.harvard.edu/flash/2021/when-correlation -does-not-imply-causation-why-your-gut-microbes-may-not-yet-be-a-silver -bullet-to-all-your-problems/.
23. Emily Oster, "The Data All Guilt-Ridden Parents Need," *New York Times*, April 19, 2019, https://www.nytimes.com/2019/04/19/opinion/sunday/baby-breastfeeding -sleep-training.html. This is a good example of confusing causation and correlation.
24. As well as spreading disease, though, this factor became less important as time went on: Oliver Burkeman, "The Diabolical Genius of the Baby Advice Industry," *Guardian*, January 16, 2018, https://www.theguardian.com/news/2018 /jan/16/baby-advice-books-industry-attachment-parenting.
25. Reed Abelson, "E.R. Doctors Misdiagnose Patients with Unusual Symptoms," *New York Times*, December 15, 2022, https://www.nytimes.com/2022/12/15 /health/medical-errors-emergency-rooms.html.
26. Kristen Panthagani, "No, ER Misdiagnoses Are Not Killing 250,000 Per Year," *You Can Know Things*, December 18, 2022, https://youcanknowthings.com /2022/12/18/no-er-misdiagnoses-are-not-killing-250000-per-year/.

9. INVESTING

1. At www.investforfree.org.
2. Joshua Franklin, "Banks Agree Near $500mn Settlement in Stock-Lending Lawsuit," *Financial Times*, August 23, 2023, https://www.ft.com/content/7fc36e60 -ab66-4c16-bcc8-2d77e08d1a57.

10. HAPPINESS

1. Still, I do wonder if he had any health insurance.
2. I hear Partner C is the worst!
3. John Clifton, *Blind Spot* (New York: Simon & Schuster, 2022); John Clifton is the CEO of Gallup, the polling organization.
4. Namely, a fairly high percentage of people reading this book, but a much lower proportion of humanity overall.
5. Susan Adams, "Unhappy Employees Outnumber Happy Ones by Two to One Worldwide," *Forbes*, October 10, 2013, https://www.forbes.com/sites/susanadams /2013/10/10/unhappy-employees-outnumber-happy-ones-by-two-to-one -worldwide/#5a4922c8362a.
6. Marie Kondo, *The Life-Changing Magic of Tidying Up* (San Francisco: Ten Speed, 2014).
7. Dave Ramsey, *The Total Money Makeover* (Nashville, TN: Nelson, 2013).
8. "Consequences of Insufficient Sleep," Healthy Sleep at Harvard Medical School, http://healthysleep.med.harvard.edu/healthy/matters/consequences.
9. Ironically, you could still die in your sleep due to a lack of sleep!
10. Simon Worral, "We Are Wired to Be Outside," *National Geographic*, February 12, 2017, https://www.nationalgeographic.com/news/2017/02/nature-fix-brain -happy-florence-williams/.
11. "Hedonic Treadmill," Wikipedia, last edited November 21, 2022, https://en .wikipedia.org/wiki/Hedonic_treadmill.
12. Jon Muth, *Zen Shorts* (New York: Scholastic, 2005).
13. Well, it was my children's parents' favorite one to read aloud, at least.
14. Melissa Chan, "Here's How Winning the Lottery Makes You Miserable," *Time*, January 12, 2016, https://time.com/4176128/powerball-jackpot-lottery-winners/.
15. Jessica Stillman, "Work, Sleep, Family, Fitness or Friends: Pick 3," *Inc.*, February 3, 2016, https://www.inc.com/jessica-stillman/work-sleep-family-fitness -or-friends-pick-3.html.
16. Danny Kahneman, one of the fathers of behavioral psychology, believes this so strongly that he will leave a vacation early if he is having a great time so that he retains this peak memory.
17. For instance, taking hundreds of pictures instead of enjoying the moment as it happens.
18. Robert Waldinger and Marc Schulz, *The Good Life: Lessons from the World's Longest Scientific Study of Happiness* (New York: Simon & Schuster, 2023).

Index

GPSR Authorized Representative: Easy Access System Europe, Mustamäe tee
50, 10621 Tallinn, Estonia, gpsr.requests@easproject.com

www.ingramcontent.com/pod-product-compliance
Lightning Source LLC
Chambersburg PA
CBHW051729260326
41914CB00040B/2031/J